Safety Leadership
and The Sense of Chronic Unease

Creating a Corporate Culture to Mitigate Risks

Nelson Oliveros

NOR Publishing LLC

For permission requests, write to:

NOR Publishing LLC
Nelson.Oliveros.KDP@gmail.com

For any consulting inquiries, write to:
NelsonOliveros@nor-c.co

This book is a work of non-fiction. All examples, case studies, and incidents described reflect either actual events, anonymized composites based on real-world scenarios, or authorial interpretation of industry dynamics. Any resemblance to specific persons or organizations is purely coincidental, unless explicitly cited.

Hardcover ISBN: 979-8-9987831-4-2
Paperback ISBN: 979-8-9987831-5-9

First edition, 2025

Dedication

To those who refuse to look the other way —
The engineers who double-check the data,
The supervisors who halt the line when something feels wrong,
The leaders who ask the hard questions when it's easier to stay silent.

To every professional who carries the invisible burden of protecting life,
not with applause, but with vigilance.

To the families behind every decision —
who trust us to bring their loved ones home safe,
Every single day.

And to those we've lost —
not just to failure, but to a failure to speak, to see, to lead.
May their memory strengthen our resolve
to build systems that serve people first.

— **Nelson Oliveros**

"The absence of accidents does not mean the presence of safety." — **Dr. James Reason**

"You never see it coming—the moment everything seems fine is often the moment before the storm." — **Anonymous Industry Operator**

"The goal is not to live forever, but to create something that does." — **Chuck Palahniuk**

Table of Content

Foreword

History shows us that major accidents, though they may be relatively rare events, can have a devastating effect on companies, their people, their reputation and share price, the surrounding communities, and the environment. Having a major accident is one of the quickest ways in which an organization can go out of business. Even at a lower level, serious incidents can have a significant impact.

My experience as a regulator and operational leader suggests that the best-run, most successful businesses are those where safety is well understood as a key ingredient of business success and where this understanding is demonstrated by the company's leadership.

Multiple studies show us that the causes of major accidents are not the result of never previously encountered phenomena or previously unseen sets of circumstances. Rather, they typically happen during day-to-day operations, and in hindsight, the warning signs were almost certainly there but not picked up or acted upon.

The major accidents that will occur somewhere in the world over the next twelve months will most likely have simple causes, a lack of operational discipline or poor engineering rigor, and it will be clear that they could have, and should have, been avoided, "If only ......"

I worked alongside the author for several years, and in his usual thoughtful style, Nelson has distilled from his own wide experience a series of real-life examples that clearly illustrate what good safety leadership looks like and the disastrous consequences that can occur when it is absent.

His book provides us with both a thought-provoking analysis and a useful practical guide for leaders seeking to make sure that their businesses remain focused and resilient.

Leaders are busy people with many competing priorities; they cannot be everywhere all the time, which means they need to transmit their concern for safety to the rest of the organization. Most importantly, they should lead by example, not just by words.

To put it another way, they must create a positive culture throughout the organization to ensure that their employees act appropriately, even during their weekend night shifts.

The safety performance of any organization is driven by its safety culture, which derives from the quality of its leadership.

It follows, therefore, that "leaders get the safety performance they deserve."

— *Chris Allen*
Former Head of HSSE at Petrofac and
Director of HSSE at Oil & Gas UK
June 2025, Aberdeen, Scotland

Preface

Across over three decades in global leadership—spanning continents, cultures, and some of the world's most complex industrial environments—I believe one truth above all others: our greatest risk is believing we're safe enough.

From petrochemical hubs in Latin America to mega-shipyards in East Asia and high-stakes offshore operations in the Caspian Sea and nearshore in Mexico, I've led through crises, cultural change, and operational transformation. But the most profound shifts I've witnessed didn't stem from technology or compliance—they came from a mindset. From leadership. From the boardroom, not just the toolbox.

While working in the Caspian region, I oversaw operations where hydrogen sulfide (H_2S)—a toxic, invisible, and instantly lethal gas—was a constant threat. Our teams relied on multiple layers of protection: advanced detection systems, escape protocols, and redundant controls. But what truly protected people wasn't just the equipment. It was a mindset: supervisors refusing to normalize deviation, engineers expecting failure, and leaders empowering teams to halt work—even at a cost. That reflexive vigilance, what I call chronic unease, is the critical difference between a near miss and a disaster. And it starts at the top.

This book is for corporate leaders—CEOs, COOs, board members, and functional executives—not just safety professionals. Because safety isn't a departmental function; it's an enterprise-wide value. In today's world of growing complexity, stakeholder scrutiny, and ESG accountability, safety leadership is business leadership.

Within these pages, you'll find more than frameworks—you'll find strategic insights. Stories and systems. Hard-earned lessons from global operations reveal how risk is created, perceived, ignored, or mitigated. You'll see how culture drives performance more powerfully than any policy. And you'll learn how chronic unease—that disciplined tension that refuses to settle for appearances—can grow from a personal mindset into a powerful organizational advantage.

This is not a technical manual. It's a leadership guide—grounded in the belief that vigilance isn't a luxury; it's a responsibility.

I invite you to read with a lens toward your own organization: not just your incident metrics, but your decision patterns. Not just your emergency plans, but your daily pressures. Where are assumptions going unchallenged? Where is silence mistaken for stability?

Because in every complex system, the seeds of failure often hide in plain sight. And those who lead with eyes wide open—who model the courage to question calmly—shape not only safer outcomes but also stronger legacies.

Bonus Insight. After Chapter 10, you'll find a supplemental chapter, co-written with Dr. Taehee Kim, an expert in mindfulness for leaders, that examines the concepts of resilience and accountability in safety leadership. It explores how mindfulness and clear accountability frameworks work together to help leaders sustain mental clarity, emotional well-being, and organizational performance under pressure.

Prologue: The Bridge Between Safety and Efficiency — Leadership, Risk, and the Culture of Vigilance

In the late 1980s, I began my career as a young safety professional—often dubbed "The Safety Guy"—in the controlled chaos of a bustling petrochemical plant. It was an era when the mantra *"Get it done TODAY!"* drowned out the quiet voice of caution. Production ruled. Caution came later—sometimes too late. It was in this high-pressure crucible that I first encountered the enduring tension between safety and efficiency—and met the mentor who would radically reshape my view of leadership.

My mentor, a battle-tested industry veteran, was blunt and unapologetically candid. In meetings, he would thunder, *"We never seem to have time to do a job right the first time, but we always find time to do it twice!"* His philosophy was clear: the pursuit of speed was too often prioritized over safety and quality.

But his most radical proposition shook the room: **eliminate the safety professionals**. Not to diminish safety—but to place full accountability with those who design and execute the work. In his view, safety should not be a siloed discipline, blamed after the fact, but a core responsibility embedded within engineering and operations. Safety wasn't a department—it was a value. A mindset.

15

This perspective challenged everything I thought I knew. Yet over time, it became clear: **true safety leadership cannot be outsourced**. A competent process engineer should not only understand how a system operates but also expect what might go wrong. They should expect failure modes, apply hazard identification methods like HAZID and HAZOP, and design with safeguards—not just efficiency—in mind. The distinction isn't between safe and unsafe jobs, but between good and poor jobs. And a good job, by definition, is one that has been, is being, and will be performed safely—always.

Decades later, despite remarkable technological and systemic advancements, the challenge persists. Safety professionals remain essential, yet too often operate in fragmented structures—where ownership is unclear, cultures are divided, and high-potential incidents lurk beneath the surface of "good enough" performance.

High-profile disasters—from Texas City to Deepwater Horizon—have propelled safety into the boardroom. Yet financial pressures still pit operational efficiency against risk reduction. Too many companies treat safety as a cost, not a strategic enabler of excellence.

But something is changing.

In recent years, the concept of chronic unease has emerged as a cornerstone of modern safety thinking. Coined by researchers like James Reason and expanded by leaders such as Dr. Todd Conklin, chronic unease describes a disciplined restlessness—a state of persistent, structured vigilance even when everything appears normal. It's grounded not in fear, but in imagination, skepticism, and critical thinking.

It asks, what might we be missing? What weak signals are we overlooking? Where is complacency creeping in?

Research shows that individuals and teams capable of sustaining chronic unease show five key traits: vigilance, a healthy sense of worry, requisite imagination, flexible mental processes, and a tendency to challenge assumptions. These aren't flaws—they're strengths. They enable us to expect problems, see the full picture, and act early to prevent escalation.

This book explores the ongoing balance between safety and efficiency—not as a binary choice, but as a leadership challenge. It argues that these forces are not mutually exclusive but interdependent. A culture that empowers vigilance, curiosity, and candor will always outperform one that silences concerns or worships productivity at all costs.

At its core are four interlocking pillars:

- **Leadership and Commitment**: Modeling expected behaviors, prioritizing risk dialogue, and placing psychological safety above political convenience.

- **Better Engineering Design**: Building systems that expect failure and absorb uncertainty—not merely optimize throughout.

- **Robust Procedures, Processes, and Systems**: Developing frameworks rooted in actual work, designed to develop rather than ossify.

- **A Strong Safety Culture**: Where every voice matters, every concern is valued, and everyone—from operator to executive—is a custodian of safety.

Imagine a workplace where supervisors start each day asking, *"What could go wrong today?"* Where engineers debate failure modes with the same rigor, they apply to optimizations. Where data is scrutinized, not for how good it looks, but for what it might conceal. Where a simple, brave act—like calling out an odd vibration in a pump—can trigger a cascade of learning and prevent disaster.

This isn't a dream. It's already happening—in pockets, in pioneering organizations, and in leaders who dare to lead differently. But it must become the norm. Because in industries where the cost of failure is measured in lives, chronic unease isn't paranoia. It's wisdom.

As you read on, you'll discover stories, models, and frameworks that bring these ideas to life. You'll learn how safety culture matures, how leadership can drive—or derail—progress, and how organizations can operationalize vigilance. You'll see how chronic unease develops from a mindset into a full-fledged operating system—one capable of transforming not just incident rates, but entire companies.

Safety isn't about avoiding risk. It's about engaging with it—intelligently, consistently, and with integrity.

And that journey begins here: with the courage to lead and the humility to stay uneasy.

Chapter 1

Why Is Strong Safety Leadership Crucial?

❖

In industries where the consequences of failure can be both immediate and catastrophic—such as oil and gas, petrochemicals, aviation, and nuclear energy—the imperative for strong safety leadership cannot be overstated. Leading in these high-stakes environments means making decisions that protect lives, preserve the environment, and maintain operational integrity.

Effective safety leadership is driven by a persistent sense of chronic unease. This is not paranoia; it is a structured mindset rooted in vigilance—a continual questioning of whether all safety measures are truly effective. As systems grow more reliable and accidents become rarer, the danger of complacency increases. It is often during these calm periods that the seeds of major incidents are unknowingly sown.

Coined by researcher Dr. Todd Conklin, *chronic unease* is the practice of assuming systems are fragile, even when they appear robust. For example, NASA's "Flight Rules"—developed after the 1967 Apollo 1 fire—require teams to revisit worst-case scenarios, regardless of past success. This principle separates good safety leaders from great ones.

My first experience with safety came long before I had ever heard of the term *safety leadership*. I was twelve years old, riding in the back seat of our family's Ford Falcon with my two younger sisters. We were driving home after visiting my uncle, and my father—who had been drinking all afternoon—was behind the wheel.

It was 11 p.m. We were crossing a five-mile bridge on a dark, quiet road. My mother sat in the passenger seat, frantically pleading with my father to slow down as he swerved between lanes. My sisters were crying, terrified by the erratic way the car zigzagged across the bridge. But as the vehicle lurched from side to side, narrowly avoiding the curb, I did something unexpected—I began assessing the risks.

I watched my father struggle to keep the car centered. My eyes shifted between the edge of the bridge and the rearview mirror, scanning for approaching headlights. Each time another car came close, I calmly warned the old man to hold steady and let them pass. My voice was measured. Though the situation was dangerous, I remained composed. We made it home safely that night. Soon after, my mother learned to drive—ensuring my father would never again drive us in such a state.

That terrifying night became the foundation of what I would later understand as *chronic unease*—a structured vigilance that underpins effective safety leadership. Three lessons from that experience have shaped my entire approach to safety:

First, I learned that panic clouds judgment, while composed vigilance can save lives. When my mother and sisters understandably panicked, I discovered a surprising ability to stay alert and focused on immediate risks. Decades later, during a petrochemical plant explosion, I would draw on this same skill—assessing hazards, prioritizing actions, and communicating with clarity under pressure.

Second, I realized that risk assessment is both systematic and intuitive. On that bridge, I wasn't following a checklist—I was a child. Yet, instinctively, I created one: scan the environment, identify immediate dangers, monitor conditions, and intervene at critical moments. That instinct developed into formal risk methodologies I've promoted ever since, always reminding teams that behind every procedure lies a human ability to detect and respond to risk.

Third, and perhaps most profoundly, I experienced how safety leadership can emerge from unexpected places. That night, the official authority figure—my father—was the greatest hazard. Meanwhile, I, the youngest present, became the de facto safety monitor. This early lesson in the democratization of safety has informed my belief that safety leadership isn't about titles—it's about awareness, courage, and the willingness to act. I've built organizations where anyone, regardless of rank, can stop unsafe work.

Twenty years later, when I conducted my first *safety culture maturity assessment* at a major process plant, I reflected on that night on the bridge. I designed the evaluation to measure not only procedural compliance but also the presence of vigilant awareness—the ability to detect danger before it manifests, to remain composed in chaos, and to speak up when it matters most.

The lessons from that night manifested in tangible ways throughout my career. The "Dynamic Risk Assessment" protocol I developed for high-hazard industries explicitly incorporates the continuous scanning technique I had instinctively used as a child. My focus on psychological safety— creating environments where team members can voice concerns without fear—stemmed from a clear realization: safety often depends on the quietest voice being heard at the most critical moment.

Even my leadership style—calm, measured, and grounded in facts rather than emotions during crises—can be traced back to that bridge. I learned that increased awareness, not increased emotion, is the key to navigating danger. This mindset proved invaluable during the ammonia plant explosion I would later witness, where a clear head amidst chaos allowed me to lead an effective emergency response.

What I couldn't articulate as a child, but understand clearly now, is that I was experiencing an ancient form of chronic unease—that persistent, healthy vigilance that refuses to be lulled by normalcy. That mindset, born on a dark bridge, would eventually form the cornerstone of my approach to safety leadership across four continents and dozens of high-risk operations.

Fast forward twelve years, and I found myself in a very different—but equally critical—situation. I had recently started working as a safety engineer at a massive petrochemical complex comprising 26 interconnected plants, producing a vast range of chemical products. The scale was immense. So were the risks.

That day, I was in my office, speaking with my family on the phone about what time I'd be home for dinner. It was a routine conversation—until a sudden explosion shattered the calm. The blast rocked the complex. The shockwave slammed into the panoramic window in front of me. Instinctively, I let the device fall. I picked it up and calmly told my wife, *"I'll be late."*

When I arrived at the scene—Train One of the ammonia plants—chaos reigned. Flames roared from a reforming gas heat exchanger. Firefighters raced to contain the blaze. The plant superintendent, severely burned but still conscious, was being escorted toward an ambulance. Even in his critical condition, he issued shutdown orders for the ammonia production facilities.

The cause of the explosion was immediately apparent: the heat exchanger had been leak-tested using process gas—a known hazardous practice and one completely out of compliance. The superintendent had overseen the procedure. It cost him dearly. Three days later, despite the efforts of medical teams, he succumbed to his injuries.

By the Numbers: The Cost of Poor Safety Leadership

- As stated by the U.S. Chemical Safety Board, 60% of major industrial accidents (2005–2020) involved failures in leadership safety practices, not just technical errors.

- The Deepwater Horizon oil spill (2010) cost $65 billion because of leadership failures (U.S. EPA).

- A strong safety culture is linked to a fivefold reduction in reportable incidents compared to weak safety cultures (UK HSE data).

The ammonia plant incident became a turning point for me. It was a stark and tragic reminder that leaders—especially those in senior positions—must model the very safety practices they expect others to follow. When leadership cannot prioritize safety, it signals that shortcuts are acceptable. In high-risk environments like petrochemicals, such compromises can have catastrophic consequences.

From the outset of my career, I've seen how production pressure can undermine safety integrity. At my first assignment in a petrochemical facility, the push to meet output targets often overshadowed conversations about risk. But one leader stood out. He began every shift with a safety briefing, consistently reminded his team that "no job is so urgent that it cannot be done safely," and empowered them to stop work if they identified a potential hazard. That culture of empowerment led to a 40% decline in incidents within two years.

Another site I visited operated in a culture where safety was a secondary concern. Meetings were rushed, near misses went unreported, and deviation from schedule was discouraged. That mindset eventually led to a preventable incident that cost the company $12 million in fines and lost production—not to mention the damage to morale and reputation.

Historical disasters like the 1988 Piper Alpha platform explosion and the 1986 Chernobyl meltdown underscore the dire consequences of deficient safety leadership. In both cases, technical failures were compounded by cultural breakdowns: on Piper Alpha, a flawed permit-to-work process and poor communication allowed a pressurized condensate leak to ignite, while at Chernobyl, ignored safety warnings and a climate of suppressed dissent led to catastrophic reactor design flaws. These events remind us that a safety-first culture cannot be a mere slogan—it must be lived and reinforced at every level through transparent decision-making, rigorous checks, and the freedom to speak up.

True safety leadership strikes a delicate balance: confidence in established systems coupled with humility about what remains unknown. Leaders must constantly ask, "What are we not seeing?" and create environments where employees feel psychologically safe to speak up. This includes:

- Walkabouts where leaders engage directly with front-line staff
- Regular safety debriefings that encourage open, honest dialogue
- Modeling behaviors that reflect a safety-first mindset

One illustrative example occurred during a refinery turnaround. A young operator noticed a strange vibration in a pump and reported it. His supervisor took the concern seriously, halted operations, and started an inspection that uncovered a failing component. The delay was minor, but the prevention of a potentially catastrophic failure was significant. This wasn't just a lucky catch—it resulted from a culture that valued chronic unease and acted on it.

Organizations must go beyond slogans like "safety first" to an operational philosophy of safety awareness. This means embedding safety into every design review, operational plan, and strategic decision. Procedures should be treated as living documents, updated with new insights, and reinforced through ongoing training and leadership involvement.

Strong safety leadership is not about rigid control—it's about influence. It's about cultivating a culture where every employee understands the value of safety, feels empowered to act, and trusts that their concerns will be taken seriously. When organizations institutionalize chronic unease and build a culture of proactive vigilance, they don't just comply with standards—they achieve resilient excellence.

Many years later, I still regret that the superintendent at the ammonia plant did not have a deeper understanding of chronic unease. But his story endures as a solemn reminder: when leaders prioritize safety in action—not just in words—they don't just prevent disaster. They create cultures where people thrive and performance excels.

Reflection for Leaders: Where in your organization might complacency be hiding behind a record of "good enough" safety performance?

Chapter 2

Understanding Safety Culture

Understanding safety culture requires moving beyond the superficial layers of procedures and compliance into the deeper dimensions of belief systems, shared values, and everyday behaviors that determine how people respond to risk when no one is watching (Reason, 1997). Culture is often described as *"how we do things around here,"* but in safety, it's more nuanced: it's about what people do when they think no one is watching and the choices they make under pressure—especially when shortcuts are tempting (Schein, 2017).

One of my early lessons came from observing two plants under the same corporate umbrella. These observations align with Hopkins' (2005) findings that organizations with identical procedures can produce radically different safety outcomes— because of culture. In one plant, there was a palpable silence— an unspoken understanding that raising safety concerns might be seen as disruptive. This mirrors what Edmondson (2019) describes as *"silent disengagement,"* where hierarchical structures suppress crucial safety communication. Conversations were clipped, feedback flowed only downward, and while people complied, they didn't believe.

At the other plant, there was a hum of open dialogue. Workers shared near misses without fear, exemplifying the *"learning culture"* described by Weick and Sutcliffe (2015) in their work on high-reliability organizations. Supervisors welcomed these disclosures, treating them not as liabilities but as learning opportunities. Leadership was present and approachable. In this plant, safety culture wasn't a program—it was a pulse.

These contrasts highlight the essence of safety culture. It is the invisible hand that shapes decisions—the collective conscience of the organization that either strengthens or undermines safety. And that's why safety culture must be cultivated intentionally—not left to chance.

When strong safety values are absent, cracks quickly appear. Complacency sets in, shortcuts become routine, and people convince themselves that "it won't happen to me." Problems go unreported, mistakes go unaddressed, and inconsistent enforcement erodes trust. In the worst cases, blame culture takes hold—focusing on assigning fault rather than solving problems. This stifles reporting and ensures that the same mistakes recur, often with devastating consequences.

I experienced this early in my career at a petrochemical company where leadership was obsessed with improving incident metrics—but through fear and blame, not genuine change. When a worker was killed in an on-site vehicle accident, the investigation revealed he hadn't worn his seatbelt and was likely distracted. Instead of exploring why safety protocols were ignored, management floated the idea that he may have suffered a heart attack. It was pure deflection—and it only deepened a culture of denial. It took years for that organization to move toward accountability and learning.

This pattern isn't unique. The 2005 Texas City refinery explosion, which killed 15 workers, was ultimately traced back to cultural failures: normalization of deviance, lack of reporting, and leadership disconnected from frontline operations. The Baker Panel Report concluded that *"the underlying causes of the tragedy were organizational and safety culture deficiencies that had existed for years."*

This example illustrates what Dekker (2016) calls the "blame cycle"—where punitive responses to incidents drive concerns underground. The Texas City case revealed identical failures: normalization of risk, poor communication, and leadership disengagement.

At the core of a strong safety culture is psychological safety— the belief that one can speak up, make mistakes, or question decisions without fear of ridicule or retaliation. This doesn't mean a lack of accountability, but an environment where accountability is constructive, not punitive.

Harvard's Amy Edmondson underscores this point. In high-performing teams, psychological safety correlates with higher reporting of near misses and concerns, which reduces the chance of catastrophic failures. In aviation, for example—where mistakes can be fatal—airlines that implemented Crew Resource Management (CRM) training, which emphasizes open communication, saw a 50% reduction in accident rates over a decade.

Leaders play a pivotal role in shaping this culture. Their behavior sets the tone. When executives prioritize safety walkarounds, genuinely listen to employee concerns, and model humility by acknowledging their own learning curves, they create space for others to do the same. Conversely, when leaders are distant, inconsistent, or dismissive, trust erodes—and fear takes its place.

Edmondson's (2018) research in healthcare found that teams with higher psychological safety reported 30% more near misses, resulting in significantly fewer serious errors. Aviation's success with CRM training (Helmreich & Merritt, 2001) further demonstrates how formalizing open communication reduces accidents.

One of the most powerful lessons I've encountered about safety leadership came from Pablo, the general manager of safety, during a monthly executive safety review following a site fatality. The atmosphere was heavy with grief and discomfort. When Pablo began, he didn't cite statistics or mask reality with euphemisms. He looked each executive in the eye and said,

"We have killed another worker this past month."

Those words stunned the room into silence. The CEO went pale, and the VP of Operations shifted uncomfortably. Legal counsel reflexively objected, "Pablo, *you can't say that. It's irresponsible.*" But Pablo stood firm.

"We need to face the reality that our decisions—our collective actions or inactions—have consequences. We cannot distance ourselves from this loss."

That moment was more than a shock—it was a crucible. The room, once tense and defensive, softened as the gravity of the moment sank in. For the first time, the executive team confronted the truth: safety is not merely a frontline issue. It reflects leadership priorities, decisions, and behaviors.

What followed marked a profound cultural shift. The CEO, visibly moved, broke the silence. *"Pablo is right. We can't hide behind process or policy. If we're truly accountable, we need to act like it."* He called for an immediate pause on all nonessential operations and convened an emergency summit to examine not just the incident but the systemic failures that made it possible.

Within days, the executive team implemented several concrete actions that rippled across the organization:

Redefining Accountability: A new safety accountability charter was adopted, clarifying that every leader—from the boardroom to the shop floor—handled their team's safety outcomes. This was not symbolic; it was a contractual commitment tied to performance reviews and bonus structures.

Leadership Visibility: Senior leaders began regular site visits and "safety walks," engaging directly with frontline workers to listen, learn, and show visible commitment. These were authentic conversations—not scripted tours—that built trust and broke down barriers.

Open Reporting and Learning: The "Speak Up for Safety" initiative was launched, encouraging employees to report hazards, near misses, and unsafe conditions without fear. Leadership clarified that reporting was a sign of vigilance, not weakness, and celebrated those who spoke up.

Policy and Training Overhaul: A full review of safety policies was conducted, with frontline employees co-writing procedures to reflect real-world conditions. Training programs were redesigned to go beyond compliance, fostering a mindset of chronic unease and proactive risk management.

Just Culture Implementation: Inspired by Pablo's candor, the company transitioned from a blame-oriented model to a *just culture*, where mistakes were opportunities for learning. Investigations shifted focus from individual error to systemic issues and leadership decisions.

The results were significant and measurable. Over the next two years:

Incident reporting increased by 40%—not because conditions worsened, but because employees trusted their voices would be heard.

Lost-time injuries fell by 50%.

Most importantly, a culture of shared responsibility and authentic accountability took root—from toolbox talks to boardroom strategy.

Pablo's once-provocative statement became a cultural touchstone. New leaders were trained using a recording of that pivotal meeting, and the phrase "We are all accountable" was engraved into the company's safety vision. The transformation wasn't instant. There were setbacks and resistance. But the shift was undeniable: safety was no longer a compliance checkbox. It was a lived value, modeled by leadership and sustained by a collective willingness to confront uncomfortable truths.

This mirrors the cultural transformation at Alcoa under CEO Paul O'Neill, who made safety his top priority. He famously halted production to address hazards—cutting injuries by 90% while tripling stock value. As O'Neill often said, *"Safety is the window into everything about your business."*

O'Neill's impact (O'Neill & Schultz, 2013) provides empirical evidence that safety-led leadership can simultaneously improve safety and profitability. His legacy embodies what Geller (2016) calls "actively caring leadership."

To guide cultural development, several models provide useful frameworks:

The Bradley Curve maps a journey from reactive (safety only after incidents) to interdependent cultures, where teams proactively care for one another.

Hudson Model adds a psychological lens, showing a progression from *pathological* (ignoring safety) to *reactive*, *calculative*, and finally *generative* cultures where safety is embedded across the organization.

The UK Health and Safety Executive (HSE) emphasizes leadership engagement, continuous learning, and improvement as pillars of strong safety cultures.

But no model can replace honest, ground-level engagement. Surveys and metrics may help assess where an organization stands, but it's the conversations—the gritty, unfiltered discussions in break rooms and job sites—that reveal the true state of culture. It's in these moments that leaders uncover not just what people do, but why they do it.

Improving safety culture demands more than slogans or policies. It requires deliberate practice: rewarding transparency, embedding reflection into routines, and making learning visible.

At one site, we began each shift with a simple "Safety Moment," where anyone—regardless of title—could share a concern, insight, or suggestion. Over time, this modest ritual transformed the tone of our meetings from passive compliance to active engagement.

Studies show the organizations implementing daily safety huddles see a 20% increase in hazard reporting within six months.

The "Safety Moment" practice aligns with recommendations from the National Safety Council (2020) for daily safety huddles. Similar approaches, such as Toyota's Andon Cord system (Liker, 2004) and Japan's Kaizen philosophy (Imai, 2012), provide cross-cultural validation of these methods—reinforcing the value of simple, repeatable behaviors that build safety into everyday work.

Another powerful tool was the "look-back–look-forward" debrief. At the end of each week, teams reflected on what had gone well, what had been a close call, and what to monitor in the days ahead. These sessions weren't mandated—they were team-owned. And because of that, they became sacred time—moments where culture wasn't just discussed but lived and reinforced through shared reflection and intent.

In Japan, this approach is deeply embedded in the Kaizen philosophy of continuous improvement. Toyota's "Andon Cord" system, where any worker can stop the production line to address a safety concern, exemplifies this mindset. The

> result? Toyota's injury rates are 80% lower than the industry
> average.

In this context, chronic unease is the undercurrent of mature safety cultures. It's the healthy tension that prevents complacency and the persistent questioning that drives improvement. When a plant hasn't had a lost-time injury in a year, do we celebrate and move on? Or do we ask, what *aren't we seeing? Are we getting lucky, or are we truly getting better?*

Embedding chronic unease means treating success as temporary and risk as dynamic. It requires recognizing that every system degrades, every process drifts, and every routine can breed blindness. It means deliberately seeking weak signals—those subtle cues that something may be off, such as a slight vibration, a skipped checklist step, or a worker's hesitation around a new procedure.

To support this mindset, leading organizations train not just for compliance but for curiosity. They run scenario drills with no tidy endings. They celebrate the reporting of near misses more than perfect metrics. And they reward those who challenge the status quo, even when it's uncomfortable.

Culture isn't static. It grows with every hire, every conversation, and every decision. A robust safety culture needs continuous investment—in leadership development, in systems that promote feedback, and in rituals that reinforce core values. But the most powerful lever is still leadership behavior. When leaders consistently walk the talk, the organization follows.

As we continue this journey, remember: culture doesn't change because we demand it. It changes because we live it—day in, day out.

In the next chapter, we'll explore how to assess where your organization sits on the safety culture maturity curve and how to take practical steps forward. You'll learn the markers of progress—and the traps that often derail it. Because the first step toward getting where you want to be is understanding where you are.

Chapter 3

Safety Culture Maturity Levels

Stepping into two different facilities—even within the same organization—can feel like entering different worlds. One hums with quiet confidence, where workers move with purpose, openly share insights, and engage in safety conversations. The other feels tense and muted, with eyes downcast and procedures followed more out of obligation than conviction. These contrasts don't just reflect differences in management style—they reflect differences in safety culture maturity.

The journey of safety culture maturity is neither linear nor uniform. It's a continuum—a climb from environments where safety is merely tolerated to ones where it is deeply embedded and valued. This chapter explores how organizations move through this maturity spectrum—and what signals show readiness for the next step.

The journey is not without obstacles. One of the biggest challenges is taking an honest look at the current state. Metrics like incident rates or compliance records can offer a false sense of security. Numbers might look good on paper, but a strong safety culture is built on more than data—it's rooted in trust, behavior, and mindset at every level.

Take, for instance, a Mexican offshore service company. Leadership believed their safety culture was exemplary—based on their impressively low incident rates. But a deeper look revealed inconsistency. Incident definitions were unclear. Data collection lacked rigor. As a result, many injuries went unreported. It wasn't malicious—just misunderstood. But it masked the actual risk.

Diego Martinez, a ten-year veteran roughneck, recalled, "For years, we never reported the minor cuts or near misses. No one told us not to—it was just understood. You wrapped a bandage around your hand and kept going." This unspoken norm created an artificial picture of safety performance—one that comforted leadership but left workers vulnerable.

When these discrepancies came to light, leadership faced a decision: defend the status quo or face uncomfortable truths. Production Manager Carlos Fuentes remembered the turning point: *"My first instinct was defensive—those numbers got us industry recognition. But after a sleepless night reviewing incident reports and employee health records, I became the biggest advocate for change."*

The transformation didn't begin with new procedures—it began with listening. Leadership held small group sessions, inviting open dialogue without fear of reprisal. Offshore Installation Manager Manuel Ortiz recalled the early silence: *"No one believed we actually wanted to hear problems. It wasn't until our platform director admitted he once ignored a gas detector alarm that the room thawed."*

That moment of vulnerable leadership broke the ice. Soon, hidden injuries were being reported. Luis Gomez, a maintenance supervisor, shared, *"When I reported three unreported hand injuries, I expected resistance. Instead, they paused operations to redesign the tool. That's when I knew it was real."*

The company refined its reporting systems—but more importantly, it changed its response. Every report received a personal leadership follow-up within 24 hours. Concern-raisers were recognized in safety meetings. When a junior engineer flagged a risky transfer procedure, he was invited to lead the redesign.

"The most powerful moment," recalled Safety Director Elena Vasquez, "was when our CEO spent three hours in one-on-one conversations with workers—no managers, no filters. He even canceled his helicopter to stay overnight and continue listening."

Supervisory training was revamped. It moved beyond incident classification to include active listening, inclusion, and psychological safety. Leadership performance evaluations were overhauled to emphasize safety engagement over production targets.

The company established a "safety council" with rotating members from all levels, ensuring that frontline workers had a voice in safety policies and decisions. During an early meeting, veteran crane operator Javier Mendez voiced his doubts: *"We've heard promises before."* The operations director didn't respond defensively. Instead, he asked, "What *would convince you we're serious this time?"* That honest exchange led to the creation of an accountability system where safety commitments were publicly tracked.

Gradually, a new atmosphere took root. Reporting stopped being seen as *"getting someone in trouble"* and started being viewed as protecting colleagues. Supervisor Antonio Cruz captured the shift: *"Now when someone stops work for a safety concern, they're treated like heroes, not troublemakers."*

Facing the truth allowed the organization to tackle deeper systemic issues. They found that excessive overtime strongly correlated with incidents, prompting a redesign of staffing models. Patterns in near-miss reports revealed design flaws in widely used equipment—triggering engineering changes across their fleet.

Two years into this transformation, a visiting industry auditor noted a visible cultural difference: *"In most companies, people tense up when safety is mentioned. Here, they lean in—eager to contribute."* Initially, incident rates rose as underreporting disappeared, prompting tough conversations with corporate leadership. But over time, serious injuries fell, and the change became undeniable.

Perhaps the most powerful signal of progress came through employee surveys. Responses to the question, *"Does management care more about safety or production?"* shifted dramatically. What had once been the company's greatest blind spot became its most authentic strength.

A 2022 study by the International Association of Oil & Gas Producers (IOGP) shows that organizations with transparent incident reporting systems experience 50% fewer severe incidents over a five-year period compared to those with opaque or punitive systems. Accurate data is key to proactively improving safety.

The takeaway? Honesty is the foundation of growth. Before setting ambitious goals or launching major initiatives, organizations must take a candid look at where they stand.

Frameworks like the Bradley Curve, the Hudson Safety Maturity Model, and the UK HSE Safety Culture Maturity Model offer valuable insights. But their true effectiveness hinges on one essential condition: a willingness to face uncomfortable truths.

A comparative analysis by the Institution of Occupational Safety and Health (IOSH) in 2023 revealed that organizations using structured maturity models progress 30% faster through the stages than those without a framework

Once you've assessed your current safety maturity level, the next step is to envision the future. This vision should inspire everyone—from top leadership to frontline workers.

Whether it's creating an environment where employees are encouraged to report hazards or fostering a culture where safety is a shared responsibility, this vision becomes a guiding star—anchoring every decision and action.

A 2021 report by the National Safety Council (NSC) found that organizations with a clearly articulated safety vision see a 35% higher employee engagement rate in safety initiatives. This highlights the power of a unifying goal in driving cultural change.

The Stages of the Bradley Curve (DuPont™ Safety Culture Model)

The Bradley Curve illustrates the evolution of workplace safety culture, showing how improved safety performance correlates with higher employee engagement and trust. Developed by

DuPont, it outlines the shift from compliance-based safety to an interdependent, values-driven culture.

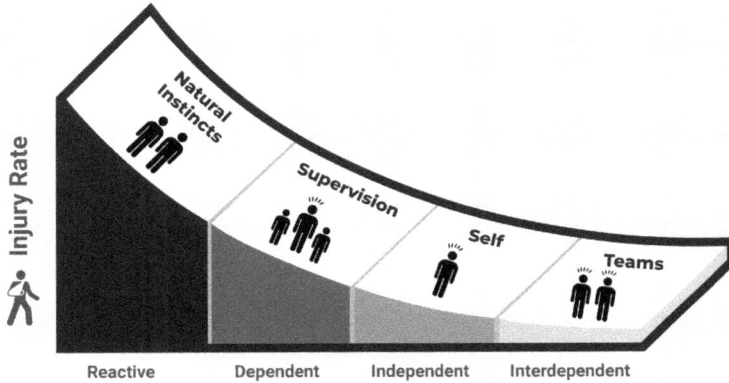

Figure 1. The Bradley Curve Safety Maturity Model

1. Reactive Stage (Dependent Culture)

Safety is viewed as a matter of luck or personal responsibility. Organizations in this stage only respond to incidents after they occur, and employees follow safety rules out of fear of punishment rather than a real understanding of risk.

Example: On a construction site I visited, workers regularly avoided reporting minor injuries out of concern for disciplinary consequences. One foreman admitted that if a worker cut their hand or twisted an ankle, they'd "walk it off" rather than face paperwork or blame. As a result, hazards accumulated unaddressed, and serious incidents became normalized.

49

Data: OSHA reports that workplaces in this stage experience three times as many recordable incidents as those in more mature safety cultures.

2. Dependent Stage (Compliance-Driven Culture)

Safety becomes procedural and rule-based. Employees comply with policies because they are expected to—not because they truly believe in them. Supervision plays a critical role, but intrinsic ownership is still missing.

Example: At a manufacturing plant, strict PPE usage was enforced. Yet, when supervisors weren't present, workers often bypassed eye protection or gloves to speed up tasks. Safety was management's job, not a shared value. When asked why they cut corners, workers cited production pressure and habit.

Data: A 2021 study in *Safety Science* found that 50% of workers in compliance-driven environments admit to bypassing safety protocols under time pressure.

3. Independent Stage (Safety as a Personal Value)

At this stage, individuals begin to internalize safety. Employees take responsibility for their own actions, speak up about hazards, and act safely even when no one is watching. Leadership still matters, but personal accountability becomes central.

Example: At a chemical plant, a technician voluntarily shut down an area of operations after detecting a strange smell that turned out to be a gas leak. He faced no retaliation and was later recognized in front of his peers. The plant's safety culture encouraged this proactive behavior as a norm.

Data: Companies operating in this stage report 60% fewer incidents than those in the dependent stage (DuPont, 2018).

4. Interdependent Stage (Collective Responsibility)

Safety becomes part of the team's identity. Everyone looks out for one another. Accountability is mutual. At this level, culture is sustained not just by individual habits but by group expectations and peer feedback.

Example: On an offshore oil rig I worked with, it was standard for anyone—regardless of rank or experience—to call out unsafe practices. During one drill, a junior crew member stopped a supervisor who was bypassing a harness check. Rather than being scolded, the supervisor praised the intervention, reinforcing the culture of collective responsibility.

Data: Organizations at this stage achieve injury rates up to 90% lower than industry averages (DuPont, 2020).

The Hudson Safety Culture Maturity Model

Developed by Professor Patrick Hudson, this model describes how organizations evolve from viewing safety as a hindrance to embracing it as a core operational value. It outlines five distinct stages.

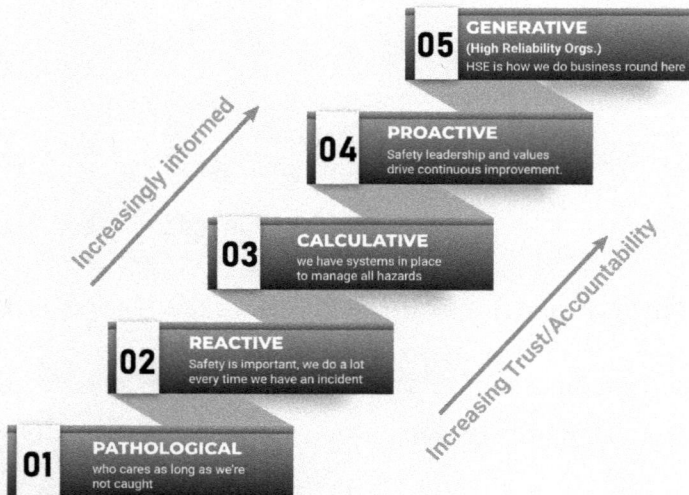

Figure 2. The Hudson Safety Maturity Model

1. Pathological Stage ("Safety as a Hindrance")

Leaders dismiss safety. Reporting is discouraged or punished. Employees protect themselves by staying silent.

Example: I encountered a manager who openly mocked internal audits, calling them a "waste of time" during a morning briefing. His attitude filtered down to the crew, who stopped reporting near misses altogether. One worker told me, "If you say something, you're the problem."

Data: The UK HSE reports that up to 70% of incidents in pathological cultures go unreported, contributing to a dangerously false sense of safety.

2. Reactive Stage ("Safety After Accidents")

Action is only taken after something goes wrong. Quick fixes are common, but sustained improvement is rare.

Example: After a significant chemical spill, one company introduced weekly safety briefings. However, within two months, attendance dropped, and previous habits returned. The changes were reactionary, not sincere.

Data: A 2020 *Journal of Safety Research* study found that 60% of reactive organizations regress within six months of a major incident.

3. Calculative Stage ("Safety by the Numbers")

Safety is managed through KPIs, audits, and formal systems— but often becomes a box-ticking exercise. Culture may appear healthy on paper, but engagement is often lacking.

Example: A logistics firm I visited had perfect documentation and completed all required inspections. Yet workers routinely bypassed procedures when rushed. One said, "We do the checklist because we have to—not because it helps."

Data: According to a 2023 Deloitte survey, 45% of employees in calculative-stage organizations see safety processes as bureaucratic hurdles.

4. Proactive Stage ("Safety as Prevention")

Organizations look ahead. Risk assessments become forward-focused. Employees feel safe raising concerns.

Example: On an offshore platform, a deckhand raised a concern about a vibration in the crane's control panel. Rather than dismiss it, the team paused work, investigated, and uncovered a developing fault. The company's culture had developed to treat every concern as valid—even if it seemed small.

Data: Proactive companies report 40% fewer recordable incidents than those in the calculative stage (ASSP, 2022).

5. Generative Stage ("Safety as a Core Value")

Safety is second nature. It informs every decision. Improvement is continuous and shared.

Example: At a European refinery, all new hires spend their first week shadowing safety mentors. A culture of curiosity and questioning is cultivated from day one. When a technician paused work because of a subtle noise in a valve, leadership didn't question the delay—they praised the instinct.

Data: Generative organizations achieve injury rates 90% below industry norms (Hudson, 2018).

The UK HSE Safety Culture Maturity Model

This framework from the UK Health and Safety Executive focuses on how deeply safety is embedded within daily behaviors and how leadership and systems reinforce maturity.

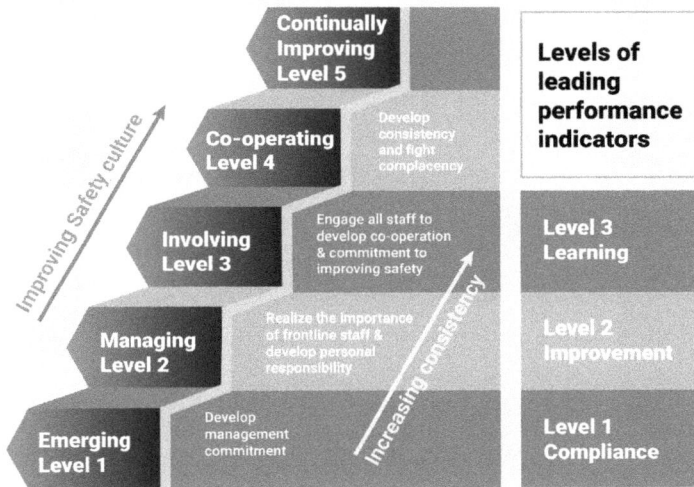

Figure 3. The UK HSE Safety Culture Maturity Model

1. Emerging (Awareness of Safety)

Safety is acknowledged but often inconsistently applied. Systems are informal and reactive.

Example: At a small warehouse, safety signage was present, but most employees hadn't been trained in how to respond to emergencies. Risk assessments were outdated or missing altogether.

Data: HSE reports that 70% of small businesses in this stage lack formal risk documentation.

2. Managing (Systems in Place)

Policies are established, but safety remains top-down. Worker engagement is minimal.

Example: A light manufacturing facility relied heavily on checklists and monthly audits. When asked for input, workers often said, "That's not my job." Safety was management's concern, not theirs.

Data: HSE findings show 40% of companies at this stage experience stagnation in safety performance because of limited worker ownership.

3. Involving (Employee Engagement)

Frontline employees actively take part. Concerns are welcomed, and improvement suggestions are implemented.

Example: In a regional hospital, nurses and technicians were invited to co-design infection prevention protocols. Their changes led to a measurable drop in contamination events.

Data: Organizations in this stage report up to 50% fewer incidents than those in the Managing stage (HSE, 2019).

4. Cooperating (Shared Ownership)

Safety becomes a team effort. Productivity and protection are balanced. Collaboration is expected.

Example: On a construction project, subcontractors and site supervisors jointly reviewed daily risk assessments. No task began until everyone understood and agreed to the control measures.

Data: HSE reports a 75% reduction in serious incidents at this level.

5. Continually Improving (Innovation & Learning)

Risk is expected, not just reacted to. Learning is ongoing, and safety practices develop constantly.

Example: An aviation firm implemented predictive analytics to identify flight line risks before incidents occurred. Based on data trends, training programs were updated monthly.

Data: Organizations at this level achieve incident rates 90% below the industry average (HSE, 2022).

Important points: Comparing the Three Models

Model	Core Focus	Progression Trigger	Peak Stage
Hudson Model	Cultural beliefs & behaviors	Shift from bureaucracy to trust	Generative (safety as instinct)
Bradley Curve	Trust & employee interdependence	Moving from rules to personal accountability	Interdependent (collective responsibility)
UK HSE Model	Structured organizational maturity	Employee engagement → continuous learning	Continually improving (innovation & adaptation)

Unified Insights for Safety Leaders

1. Compliance isn't enough. All models show that rules alone fail without trust and engagement (e.g., calculative vs. generative/interdependent stages).

2. Culture beats systems. The highest-performing organizations—Generative, Interdependent, or Continually Improving—treat safety as a shared value, not just a policy.

3. Regression is a risk. Without continuous effort, companies can slide backward, especially after major incidents (reactive stage pitfalls).

4. Listening to employees helps a company compete better. When employees freely share concerns and report issues proactively, incidents decrease by 40–60%.

But identifying where you are on these maturity ladders is just the beginning. True cultural maturity is measured not only by audits and metrics but also by daily behaviors and conversations—how close calls are handled, how feedback is delivered, and how leadership reacts to bad news.

I recall a refinery supervisor who, after a near miss, simply asked his team, "What *do we need to do differently?*" That single question opened a floodgate of insights—latent frustrations, procedural gaps, and design flaws. By listening, he transformed risk into opportunity.

> A 2021 Gallup poll found that teams with open communication channels report 25% more near misses, providing critical data for preventive action.

Moving up the maturity curve requires deliberate leadership—rooted in curiosity, humility, and a willingness to revisit long-held norms. Leaders must ask more than they tell and listen more than they speak.

Some organizations embed this through rituals:

- "Learning Circles": Weekly discussions on safety wins and worries

- "Pause Points": Built-in moments to reassess conditions during high-risk tasks

Over time, these practices normalize vigilance, reinforce psychological safety, and humanize safety systems.

> Research from the Harvard Business Review (2023) shows that organizations with regular reflection practices see a 20% improvement in safety performance year over year.

Where does your organization stand today? More importantly, where do you want to go? And what small, specific leadership behavior can you change today to move in that direction?

Progress isn't linear. Leadership turnover, cost pressures, and setbacks can cause backsliding. But sustained maturity comes from knowing that culture is like muscle—it needs consistent exercise. And chronic unease is not fear—it's the mindset that drives resilience.

In the next chapter, we will explore the strategies and interventions that help organizations shift their culture deliberately: the leadership behaviors, communication tools, and operational changes that turn aspiration into action.

Reflection Question:

Which framework resonates most with your organization's journey?   *Why?*

Where does your organization sit today? What one behavior change could you champion tomorrow to move forward?

Chapter 4

Improving Safety Culture Maturity

✤

Improving safety culture maturity is not a matter of luck—nor is it the result of well-written policies alone. It is an intentional journey requiring vision, commitment, and, above all, leadership that walks the talk. Organizations do not stumble into mature safety cultures—they build them, one behavior, one decision, and one conversation at a time.

Leadership powers transformation. Not merely positional authority, but influence that spans departments, functions, and hierarchies. I've seen how one leader can shift an entire culture—someone who steps out of the office and into the field, listens before speaking, and asks questions not to test but to understand. At one manufacturing facility, the CEO began each week with a safety walkthrough. He wasn't inspecting—he was engaging. He asked operators what had concerned them that week, what near misses they'd observed, and what improvements they'd suggest. Over time, this practice became a cultural cornerstone, with employees proactively sharing insights and solutions.

This kind of leadership creates psychological permission—to care, to speak up, and to intervene. When employees truly believe that safety is valued—not just as a slogan, but as a lived practice—they internalize it. They act not because they're told to, but because they want to.

Leadership expert Jordan Peterson, in his book "12 Rules for Life," wrote, "Standing tall with your shoulders back means accepting life's heavy responsibilities." This metaphor underscores leadership's essence: owning responsibility with resilience and authenticity. Effective safety leadership doesn't stem from technical skill alone—it draws from moral strength and character. In moments of pressure, ethical conviction becomes the anchor for trust and transformation.

I witnessed this myself while overseeing an offshore plant in Mexico amidst a turbulent company transition. The company I worked for was selling its operations to a French firm known for shaky ethical practices. From the outset, I resolved to uphold the values I'd carried throughout my career.

Soon after starting, my new supervisor began pressuring me to compromise safety, use aggressive tactics with clients, and prioritize speed over integrity. I refused. I explained my stance, escalated when necessary, and bore the consequences. The pressure was intense. But trust and integrity were non-negotiable. I would not sacrifice the credibility of my team—or myself—for short-term advantage.

Ultimately, I was released two months before the transition ended. It was framed as a "business decision," but I knew the truth. I left with my head high, knowing I had done the right thing. Less than a year later, the company severed ties with that same client—a reminder of the cost of prioritizing shortcuts over values.

That experience taught me leadership isn't about avoiding conflict—it's about doing what's right, especially when it's hard. When leaders hold to personal integrity over convenience, they inspire others to do the same. In safety culture, trust is the foundation, and without it, no initiative can succeed.

A key driver of cultural maturity is a clearly articulated, resonant safety vision. This vision must go beyond aspiration—it must reflect the realities of the work environment. The language should mirror that of the workforce, drawing from their experiences and challenges. In some of the most successful companies I've worked with, safety visions were co-created with employees—from engineers to custodians.

These visions gained traction because they addressed frontline concerns, making them believable and actionable. One mining company, for example, developed the vision *"Zero Harm, Every Shift"* through frontline workshops, ensuring it reflected daily risks and routines.

From vision comes mission—the concrete roadmap for how the vision will be achieved. The mission defines priorities, sets goals, and communicates expectations across the organization. Whether it's reducing near-miss incidents by 40% or conducting safety dialogues on every shift, a strong mission transforms intention into action. One oil and gas company I advised embedded safety into career advancement metrics, aligning personal growth with cultural maturity.

Next comes strategy: a focused safety plan that identifies high-risk areas, allocates resources, and sets clear milestones. Avoid vague ambitions like *"we want to improve."* Instead, specify what will change, who will lead it, and the timeline for delivery.

At a global logistics firm, transformation began with site-level hazard mapping. Cross-functional teams—warehouse operators, technicians, and dispatchers—worked together to identify daily risks. That map informed precise interventions: rerouting traffic, updating signage, redesigning lifting techniques, and more. Each success had a champion and was shared widely. Within 18 months, recordable incidents fell by 60%, proving the power of collaborative, data-driven change.

Education and communication are the twin engines of any transformation. Training must be continuous, interactive, and relevant. Too often, training is generic and detached from actual work. But when it includes actual scenarios, peer learning, and worker stories, it sticks.

At a chemical plant in Germany, traditional lectures were replaced with immersive simulations. The result? A 45% increase in hazard recognition.

Feedback is equally vital. Mature organizations embed mechanisms for ongoing employee input—through hotlines, surveys, suggestion boxes, and open forums. One company created a weekly "feedback hour," where employees met directly with supervisors. Not all suggestions were adopted—but all were heard. Over time, this led to 200+ employee-driven improvements, reinforcing a culture of shared ownership.

Metrics matter, too—but mature cultures look beyond lagging indicators like injury rates. They focus on leading indicators:

- Participation in safety observations
- Timeliness of corrective actions
- Frequency of safety interactions
- Training engagement

Displaying these transparently—on dashboards, in break rooms, or at town halls—fosters collective ownership. A Canadian construction firm saw a 30% increase in safety engagement after launching a live dashboard tracking near misses and response actions.

Case studies offer powerful lessons. DuPont, for example, used the Bradley Curve to track cultural progression, linking specific leadership actions to shifts in safety behavior. BP, post-Texas

City, launched a global leadership program emphasizing risk literacy and emotional intelligence, which reduced serious incidents by 75% over five years. Shell integrated its safety systems with real-time data dashboards, allowing supervisors to adjust protocols on the fly. Wood Group embedded safety supports into every project team, decentralizing ownership and improving safety performance by 50% across its global operations.

In all these examples, the common thread is leadership commitment, systemic strategy, and cultural alignment. Success is not defined by the absence of incidents alone, but by the presence of vigilance.

Positive reinforcement is another cornerstone. I've seen dramatic shifts when organizations began publicly recognizing small safety acts. One company launched "Catch of the Month," spotlighting employees who reported near misses or proposed practical safety improvements. These recognitions weren't perfunctory; they were stories shared in newsletters and meetings. They became culture carriers. Over time, this initiative led to a 40% increase in near-miss reporting, turning potential incidents into learning opportunities.

Improvement also requires sustained attention. Culture is not static. It is influenced by new hires, economic cycles, leadership turnover, and external pressures. Periodic assessments—conducted by neutral facilitators—can help recalibrate efforts.

These assessments should combine surveys, focus groups, and observational studies. They must explore not just compliance but engagement: Do employees feel heard? Do they trust their supervisors? Are they proud of the safety record? A lithium extraction company I worked with conducted bi-annual culture audits, using the insights to refine their strategies and maintain momentum.

As Jordan Peterson asserts in *12 Rules for Life*, "Compare yourself to who you were yesterday, not to who someone else is today" (Peterson, 2018). This principle resonates in safety culture, where the goal is continuous improvement, not perfection. Metrics like incident rates and near misses provide valuable insights, but they often cannot capture the nuances that qualitative feedback can uncover. For instance, at one manufacturing firm, anonymous surveys revealed widespread confusion about hazard signage, prompting leadership to overhaul their communication strategy. Continuous monitoring is vital for sustaining improvements. Regular evaluations help identify what's working, what needs change, and where additional risks may arise. However, trust is equally important. Employees must believe that the data collected shall be used to improve processes, not punish individuals.

Improving safety culture maturity is about more than policies or metrics—it's about values, trust, and ethical leadership. Leaders must model the change they want to see, championing a culture where safety is second nature. By crafting a clear vision, executing actionable strategies, and building trust at every level, organizations can create not only safer workplaces but also stronger, more resilient communities.

Ultimately, the maturity of a safety culture is best measured by its resilience to adversity. In the wake of an incident, does the team unite to learn from it or assign blame? When procedures change, is there resistance or adaptation? When an additional risk emerges, do people raise the alarm or stay silent? A notable example is NASA's response to the Columbia disaster, where the agency transformed its culture from one of complacency to one of relentless curiosity and transparency, ensuring that lessons from failure were institutionalized.

Leaders at every level must remember: the goal is not perfection, but progress. Not to eliminate all risk, but to embed a reflexive, system-wide capacity to see, respond, and grow. Chronic unease, in this context, is the ongoing tension that keeps us alert—not fearful, but aware; not anxious, but committed.

As we transition to the next chapter, we'll shift our focus to the systems that support this transformation. Management systems—like ISO 45001—provide the framework for aligning vision with action, strategy with behavior, and intention with measurable outcomes. They are not ends in themselves but scaffolding for the culture we seek to build.

Chapter 5

Management Systems for Safety

In many organizations, safety management systems (SMS) are perceived as dense documents filed away on shared drives—referenced only during audits or inspections. But in mature, high-performing cultures, the SMS is not a binder gathering dust. It is a breathing framework that integrates safety into the fabric of daily operations. It aligns vision with action, connects strategy with behavior, and provides structure to vigilance.

To move from simply following rules to actively managing safety, we must rethink what a safety management system truly is. At its core, an SMS is a structured set of policies, procedures, and practices designed to manage risks systematically, ensure compliance, and promote continuous improvement. But that definition alone is insufficient. A truly effective SMS is one that people use, trust, and help to grow.

One of the most transformational SMS implementations I witnessed took place at a large chemical plant. Prior to adopting the system, safety was the exclusive domain of the HSE team. Operators followed procedures but rarely questioned them. Audits focused on paperwork rather than behaviors. After the organization implemented an ISO 45001-aligned system, that dynamic changed. Safety became a shared responsibility. Cross-functional teams were trained in risk assessments, and feedback loops were embedded into routine workflows.

The leadership team made a pivotal decision: they integrated safety metrics into business performance dashboards. This wasn't symbolic—it ensured that safety had equal standing alongside production, cost, and quality. Operational decisions no longer occurred in silos. Trade-offs were debated. Risks were expected. Unintended consequences surfaced early. Safety became strategic.

A study by the National Safety Council (NSC) found that organizations integrating safety metrics into executive dashboards saw a 35% reduction in recordable incidents within two years. This underscores the importance of aligning safety with business objectives.

A study by the National Safety Council (NSC) found that organizations integrating safety metrics into executive dashboards saw a 35% reduction in recordable incidents within two years. This underscores the importance of aligning safety with business objectives.

Core Components of an SMS

Policy

The policy must be clear, endorsed at the highest level, and communicated widely. It should declare safety as a value—not just a priority—and outline the principles that guide behavior. For example, DuPont's "Safety as a Core Value" policy has helped achieve industry-leading performance, with incident rates 50% lower than the industry average.

Planning

Planning involves identifying risks and legal obligations, setting objectives, and allocating resources. Effective planning includes stakeholder input and reflects a deep understanding of operational realities. In one mining operation, planning teams included union representatives, equipment operators, and maintenance leads—ensuring that the plans weren't just top-down directives but co-created commitments.

Research by the Occupational Safety and Health Administration (OSHA) highlights that organizations involving frontline workers in safety planning reduce workplace injuries by up to 30%.

Implementation

Implementation turns plans into action. This includes training, communication, documentation, and operational controls. But more importantly, it involves engaging hearts and minds. I've seen the difference between a training session that ticks boxes and one that invites real dialogue. When people understand not just what to do but why it matters—and how it connects to their daily risks—they become stewards of the system.

A case study from BP's Texas City refinery showed that interactive, scenario-based training reduced human error-related incidents by 40% compared to traditional lecture-style sessions.

Evaluation

Evaluation is where many systems falter. Audits become exercises in paper-chasing, and feedback is filtered to avoid conflict. Mature systems, however, embrace transparency. They use a mix of internal audits, third-party assessments, and real-time data to identify strengths and weaknesses. At one logistics firm, leaders made a point of publicly sharing audit findings—not to shame, but to learn. Trends were tracked over time, and teams celebrated when improvements held.

According to a report by the International Association of Oil & Gas Producers (IOGP), companies that prioritize transparent evaluation achieve 25% faster corrective action implementation.

Continual Improvement

Continual improvement is the heartbeat of the system. It means not only fixing problems but also continuously seeking opportunities to improve. It involves learning from incidents, reviewing objectives, and adapting to change. Technology plays an increasingly important role here. With digital platforms, organizations can analyze trends, predict emerging risks, and customize interventions. Yet no software can replace the human element—the leader who asks, "What's not on this report that we need to address?"

A study by McKinsey & Company found that organizations leveraging predictive analytics in their SMS reduced near-miss incidents by 45% over three years.

International standards like ISO 45001 offer valuable structure. They emphasize leadership involvement, worker participation, risk-based thinking, and integration with other management systems. Many organizations also draw on national frameworks, such as ANSI Z10 or CSA Z1000. What matters is not the label but the intent: systems must support the culture you are building—not replace it.

For example, after adopting ISO 45001, Alcoa reported a 60% reduction in lost-time injuries within five years, showcasing the tangible benefits of a well-implemented standard.

Leadership and SMS Integration

Integrating leadership with systems is essential. Too often, leaders delegate the SMS to technical experts and focus on performance metrics alone. But when leaders walk the floor, engage with workers, and use SMS data to inform decisions, they send a powerful message. I once observed a senior executive pause a quarterly meeting to address a safety concern flagged in a pre-shift report. That moment reverberated through the organization, reinforcing that safety is not a task—it is a core business process.

A Harvard Business Review study found that companies where leaders actively took part in safety initiatives had 50% higher employee engagement in safety programs.

The benefits of a well-implemented safety management system aren't just theoretical—they're financial. Early in my career, I was tasked with coordinating an audit to assess the insurance premium for a large petrochemical complex. Historically, these audits had been unproductive. The approach was reactive: auditors asked questions, and the team scrambled to provide answers—often with mixed results.

To change the situation, I teamed up with the company's insurance department to create a plan that addressed problems before they occurred. Instead of waiting for the auditors to lead, we took control. We presented a detailed report that highlighted our successes—showcasing the systems and processes we had implemented and the measurable improvements they had delivered. We also addressed areas where we were underperforming, explaining why issues had arisen and outlining the measures we were taking to address them.

This level of transparency, rooted in the principles of ISO management systems, transformed the conversation. The auditors were impressed by our control over the situation and the clear steps we were taking to reduce risk. The result? A $5 million reduction in the insurance premium compared to previous years. It proved that clear, well-documented processes are not just profitable—they're powerful.

Implementing standards like ISO 45001 is not without its challenges. While the frameworks themselves are robust, their success depends on how they're applied. Too often, organizations focus on appearances—crafting pristine documentation to satisfy auditors—while neglecting the real-world applicability of their systems.

I've seen this firsthand. In one organization, an "army" of employees was dedicated to maintaining the documentation required for certification. Entire teams worked tirelessly to ensure that procedures, forms, and policies were flawlessly presented during audits. Yet, when I visited the field, those documents weren't being used effectively. Workers weren't familiar with the procedures, supervisors weren't enforcing them, and the systems were disconnected from day-to-day operations.

The auditors, many of whom had little field experience, were complicit in this cycle. Their focus was on the paperwork, rarely venturing into the workplace to observe practices or interview workers. This approach led to recommendations that prioritized neatness over effectiveness, perpetuating a system that looked good on paper but failed to deliver meaningful improvements in safety performance.

Breaking this cycle requires leadership. It requires a willingness to look beyond the audit and ask the hard questions: Are these systems working? Are they making our people safer? Are they solving actual problems—or just creating the illusion of progress?

Auditing for Learning, Not Just Compliance

Audits are a vital component of any safety management system, but their value depends on how they're conducted. When audits are seen as a learning opportunity rather than a compliance exercise, they become a powerful tool for growth.

I recall one audit where we flipped the script. Instead of focusing solely on the documentation, we invited the auditors to spend time in the field. They observed operations, interviewed workers, and saw firsthand how our systems operated. This approach revealed insights that would never have emerged from paperwork alone, helping us address hidden risks and strengthen our processes.

Audits should be about more than passing a test—they should be about making the organization safer. When done right, they provide a roadmap for continuous improvement, ensuring that systems develop to meet new challenges.

Feedback loops within an SMS should be tight, dynamic, and actionable. Near-miss reports, hazard observations, and safety conversations should not disappear into spreadsheets. They should inform decisions, guide training, and shape policy. In high-performing systems, these inputs are reviewed weekly, and responses are shared openly. This reinforces trust and fosters a learning culture.

Auditing, when done well, is a developmental tool. Progressive organizations have shifted from fault-finding to appreciative inquiry. Instead of asking, "Where did we fail?" they ask, "Where are we learning?" I worked with an airline that embedded learning-oriented audits into its SMS. Audit teams included peer reviewers from other locations, and their findings were not scored but synthesized into improvement plans. As a result, safety performance improved—but so did collaboration and morale.

Chronic Unease: The Mindset of Vigilance

Chronic unease is the last layer that binds the SMS together. It is the mindset that prevents systems from becoming static. Even the most mature system can become a ritual if it is not constantly questioned. That's why organizations must build in rituals of reflection—safety stand-downs, "what if" reviews, and scenario planning. These practices challenge assumptions and surface latent risks.

In one refinery, daily "Pause and Reflect" meetings were introduced. Before every shift, teams revisited a near-miss, discussed lessons learned, and explored what might go wrong today. Over time, these five-minute sessions became cultural anchors. They reminded people that vigilance is not just a response to incidents—it is a discipline.

A study by the Chemical Safety Board (CSB) found that organizations practicing chronic unease through regular reflection sessions reduced process safety incidents by 33%.

An SMS is not a silver bullet. But when designed with intention, supported by leadership, and driven by curiosity, it becomes a powerful enabler of cultural maturity. It changes safety from dealing with problems after they happen to preventing them beforehand. It turns compliance into commitment. And it ensures that no matter how good today's results may look, the organization keeps asking, what *more can we do? What are we missing?*

In the next chapter, we will explore how this structured thinking extends into risk analysis and management—where chronic unease becomes operationalized into hazard identification, control strategies, and informed decision-making.

Chapter 6

Risk Analysis and Management

❖

In high-hazard industries, managing risk is not a peripheral task—it is the core discipline upon which every other function rests. Unlike fields where consequences unfold slowly, sectors such as oil and gas, aviation, mining, and chemicals deal in real-time volatility. One lapse in attention, one faulty assumption, or one missed signal can cause irreversible damage—loss of life, environmental catastrophe, or the complete failure of a business unit.

Understanding risk means accepting its inevitability. No system is perfect, and no operation is risk-free. The goal is not to eliminate all risk—an impossible pursuit—but to recognize it early, mitigate it intelligently, and respond to it decisively. This is where risk analysis and management come into play.

The Four Pillars of Risk Management

1. Identification

Effective risk management starts with identification. It is about seeing around corners. On one offshore platform I worked with, the operations team conducted quarterly "risk foresight sessions." These were not regulatory drills; they were explorations of what might go wrong. Teams mapped operations step by step, identifying vulnerabilities that could escalate into crises. For example, during one session, a technician raised concerns about corrosion in a rarely inspected pipeline section. Further investigation revealed significant wear, averting a potential rupture.

2. Prevention

Prevention is often misunderstood as avoiding risk altogether. It's about installing barriers—physical, procedural, and cultural—that catch hazards before they turn into incidents. In a gas-processing facility, moving emergency shut-off valves after a minor incident turned a reactive fix into a preventive redesign. The new layout shaved off response time by seconds—seconds that could mean the difference between containment and disaster. Another example comes from aviation, where redundant systems and rigorous maintenance protocols prevent single-point failures from escalating into catastrophes.

3. Preparation

Preparation assumes that barriers may fail and asks, "Are we ready?" Tabletop exercises, emergency drills, and scenario planning—these are not box-checking events. When done well, they simulate pressure, reveal gaps, and strengthen muscle memory. I once witnessed a facility respond to a real chemical leak with astonishing composure—not because the scenario was anticipated, but because the response had been rehearsed, questioned, and refined. The 2010 Chilean mining accident rescue is another testament to preparation. Despite the odds, a meticulously planned operation saved 33 trapped miners, showcasing the power of preparedness.

4. Protection

Protection, the last layer, encompasses personal protective equipment, emergency response systems, and crisis communication protocols. These are the last line of defense. When all else fails, they save lives. In one case, an explosion in a polymer plant was mitigated by an automated fire suppression system and a well-practiced shelter-in-place plan. No lives were lost—not because of luck, but because of preparation. Similarly, the Fukushima nuclear disaster highlighted the critical role of protection measures, albeit with tragic lessons about the need for redundancy in emergency systems.

A suite of analytical tools supports these methodologies: **HAZID, HAZOP, BOWTIE, FMEA, JSA, LOPA**, and **QRA**. Each serves a distinct purpose, and together, they form a web of resilience.

1. **HAZID (Hazard Identification)** invites a wide-angle view. Cross-disciplinary teams walk through the process and brainstorm potential hazards. The strength of

HAZID lies in diversity—when engineers, operators, and maintainers come together, blind spots diminish. At a refinery, a maintenance worker noted that a rarely used valve could become a single point of failure during an emergency shutdown.

2. **HAZOP (Hazard and Operability Study)** dives deep. It challenges every aspect of a process using structured guidewords. In one session, the phrase "no flow" led to discovering a mislabeled valve that had escaped attention for years.

3. **FMEA (Failure Modes and Effects Analysis)** narrows the focus. It examines how individual components might fail and what impact those failures would have. At a nuclear plant, FMEA identified a backup cooling pump's vulnerability to power surges, prompting a redesign.

4. **JSA (Job Safety Analysis)** grounds the process in daily reality. By breaking down tasks into steps and analyzing each for hazards, JSA empowers teams to take ownership. On a construction site, a JSA revealed crane operation risks, resulting in new protocols and targeted training.

5. **LOPA (Layer of Protection Analysis)** quantifies risk and helps teams understand the strength and independence of safety barriers. One LOPA analysis revealed that two separate barriers shared a common

power source—a hidden vulnerability that was promptly addressed.

6. **Bowtie Analysis** bridges hazard identification and risk control by visualizing a full risk scenario in one diagram. One side shows potential causes (like human error or equipment failure), the center marks the critical event, and the other side maps consequences and safeguards. In one workshop, the team realized their entire response strategy relied on a single control room operator. The Bowtie exposed this, leading to the installation of automated isolation valves and cross-training responders.

7. **QRA (Quantitative Risk Assessment)** assigns numbers to uncertainty. It models worst-case scenarios—blowouts, vapor cloud explosions, toxic releases—and translates them into probabilities and consequences. One QRA at a chemical storage site showed shelters were inadequate for a rare but devastating scenario. Initially met with resistance, the data ultimately drove investment in more robust protection measures.

Risk management also demands cultural alignment. Technical tools alone do not prevent accidents. People must be encouraged to think critically, voice concerns, and challenge assumptions. Leaders play a pivotal role here. They must model curiosity, celebrate dissent, and reward vigilance.

I recall a refinery supervisor who, after a near miss involving a miscommunicated handover, started every shift meeting with a simple question: "What could go wrong today?" That question changed everything. It shifted the tone from compliance to engagement. Soon, operators began bringing forward scenarios and proposing safeguards. The result wasn't just fewer incidents—it was greater ownership.

Leadership and Process Safety Management: Insights from José A. Rodriguez

In the wake of BP's Macondo disaster, the U.S. Chemical Safety Board noted that, "In the wake of a disaster, immediate responders get the attention, despite underlying issues in systemic safety culture and organizational practices being the root cause." A graduate peer and trusted coach in our Loss Prevention Master's program, Rodríguez insists that genuine risk management must originate at the top of the organization and radiate outward—never the other way around.

He applies High-Reliability Organization principles, arguing that leaders need a unified vision, empowering all employees to identify and challenge weak signals before they escalate. It isn't enough to tack on corrective actions; the integrity of each barrier—from design reviews to emergency drills—must be guaranteed as a core operational element. As he says, "When leadership treats risk reduction as optional, latent failures line up like dominos—waiting for the slightest push."

Rodríguez views Deepwater Horizon and Texas City not as aberrations, but as inevitable outcomes of fragmented decision-making, ignored expertise, and discouraged dissent. "No single operator caused Macondo," he reminds us. "But a chain of poor choices and stifled warnings set the stage." His counsel is clear: process safety leadership demands more than technical fixes—it requires unwavering commitment to learning, deference to frontline expertise, and swift, decisive action when warning signs appear.

Long before Macondo, a similar confluence of poor design decisions and broken permit-to-work controls led to the 1988 Piper Alpha platform explosion in the North Sea. There, gas-compression modules had been retrofitted too close to living quarters, and a hand-tightened blind flange was left unverified—setting the stage for a condensate leak that would ignite within minutes. Piper Alpha's root causes echo the same lack of chronic unease that surfaced again at Macondo, underscoring that complacency in process safety remains deadly.

The above shall remind us that integrating process safety into performance metrics, boardroom decisions, and shift handovers transforms it from a checklist into a shared commitment. Protecting people and communities becomes everyone's responsibility.

One of my most memorable experiences in risk management occurred at the El Tablazo Petrochemical Complex in Venezuela, near Lake Maracaibo. This sprawling facility, with multiple chemical plants and high-pressure pipelines, bordered the town of El Hornito, home to nearly 2,000 residents.

Concerns grew over toxic fumes and the potential drift of gas clouds into the town. Our assessment confirmed that El Hornito lay in a direct danger zone. We modeled worst-case scenarios— gas leaks, explosions, fires—and the conclusion was clear: the town needed to be moved.

What stood out was leadership's response. They didn't just approve of the study and walk away. They pushed for funding, collaborated with local authorities, and ensured the relocation was handled ethically and responsibly. The outcome was a 300-meter buffer zone, transformed into a green belt with trees and livestock.

We later applied lessons from El Hornito to the José Azoátegui Petrochemical Complex in eastern Venezuela. Here, the risk was not a residential area but a major highway that ran dangerously close to the facility. Thousands of vehicles—including tankers—passed daily. Through rigorous assessment and leadership support, the highway was successfully moved several kilometers away, dramatically reducing the risk of a catastrophic event.

But not all risk assessments are welcomed. Sometimes they surface inconvenient truths—issues that require costly investment or tough decisions.

I encountered this during an assessment for an MTBE plant. The findings were alarming: safety gaps, weak emergency response plans, and serious containment concerns. Before I presented the report, the project manager requested a private review. After seeing the risks, he asked, "Can you adjust some of these conclusions? If we present them as-is, we'll have to invest more, which will delay the project."

I refused. Altering the findings would have compromised safety and put lives at risk. Despite the potential fallout, I stood firm. The safety investments were made. It was a powerful reminder that leadership integrity in risk management is non-negotiable.

Continuous Improvement and Chronic Unease

Continuous improvement is the backbone of risk management. This means reassessing hazards regularly, openly reviewing incidents, and maintaining relentless curiosity. Thriving organizations never assume their systems are "done." They revisit risk assessments annually or after any operational change. Their monitoring focuses on leading, not lagging, indicators. They host learning reviews, not just post-incident briefings. And even in periods of calm, they ask, "What are we learning?"

At one facility, we started a routine called "What If Wednesday." Each week, a different team proposed a hypothetical failure: "What if we lost power mid-transfer?" "What if a contractor misunderstood the permit?" These conversations built analytical capacity. Teams stopped just performing tasks—they started thinking like systems engineers.

Chronic unease is the emotional core of this discipline. It is the refusal to be lulled by quiet months or clean dashboards. It's the voice that asks, "What's hiding in plain sight?"

The next chapter examines how this vigilance extends to daily routines: leaders maintaining awareness, organizations remaining alert even when all seems well, and safety becoming a daily practice rather than a mere reaction.

Chapter 7

The Sense of Chronic Unease

✤

Creating and sustaining a state of chronic unease means cultivating a disciplined restlessness—a refusal to settle into comfort even when everything appears to be running smoothly. In high-risk industries such as oil and gas, construction, and healthcare—where the consequences of a single lapse can be catastrophic—this mindset becomes not just valuable but essential. At home, we live by these principles daily. For example, we baby-proof furniture, check the stove, and teach our children street safety. Each minor act of foresight—born of a gentle skepticism toward "all clear"—sharpens the muscle memory we bring to the plant floor or the rig.

Chronic unease is neither fear nor anxiety for its own sake, but a professional discipline rooted in resilience thinking. As Karl Weick and Kathleen Sutcliffe explain, it springs from a preoccupation with failure and a reluctance to simplify. Instead of accepting green dashboards as proof of safety, leaders and workers alike ask, "What are we not seeing?" and "What could go wrong next?" These questions turn silence into signal and routine into a source of insight. The concept is backed by psychological research: Fruhen, Flin & McLeod (2014) identify five core traits—vigilance, a propensity to worry, healthy pessimism, requisite imagination, and flexible thinking—that underpin this state of mind. These aren't negative characteristics, but wisdom in disguise: worry prompts us to engage with potential threats, imagination allows us to visualize worst-case scenarios, and flexible thinking readies us to revise assumptions when new information appears.

Origins of the Term "Chronic Unease"

The label "chronic unease" is often attributed to James Reason, a pioneer in human factors and organizational accident causation. In his 1997 work, Reason showed how repeated success can cause even experienced professionals to overlook hidden risks. He coined the term to capture a state of continuous alertness—an ingrained habit of questioning rather than accepting the status quo. Reason's work builds on the Swiss Cheese Model. He argues that organizations must address seemingly minor issues to prevent catastrophes caused by hidden failures.

Below is a graph illustrating the "Tolerance of Chronic Unease":

Chronic Unease Tolerance

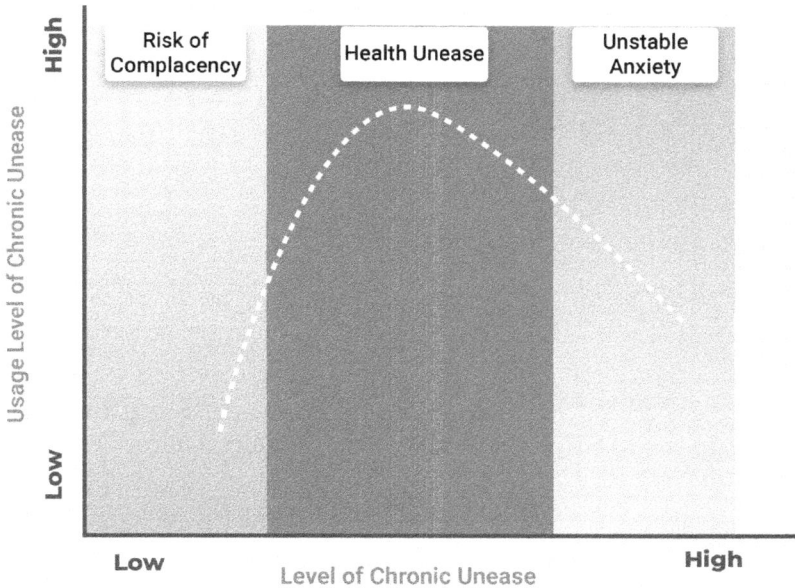

Fruhen, L., Flin, R. & McLeod, R. (2014) Chronic unease for safety in senior managers.

Figure 4. The Chronic Unease Tolerance Graph.

This curve shows that too little unease leads to complacency, where risks go unnoticed—and too much unease can trigger paralysis or avoidant behavior. The optimal zone lies in the middle range, where vigilance is high but balanced by confidence in skills and systems. When things are going well, teams can respond quickly to weak signals while still taking the initiative. As individuals grow familiar with the discomfort of doubt, their tolerance widens, allowing them to sustain chronic unease over longer periods without cognitive overload.

Embedding Chronic Unease Across the Organization

The organizational challenge lies in embedding this mindset at every level. Top leadership must model unease by leading "listening tours" and opening each meeting with questions such as, "What recent near miss surprised you?" Supervisors sustain it by walking the floor daily, pausing work when a tool is misplaced, or publicly acknowledging the smallest act of vigilance. Frontline teams bring it to life through scenario-based drills that sharpen judgment and through peer-to-peer accountability that gives everyone permission to speak up. Contractors and temporary staff experience a disproportionate number of serious incidents. Therefore, they must be fully integrated into safety programs from the start. This includes joint inductions, mentoring, and access to the same reporting and recognition systems as permanent staff.

Chronic unease does come with trade-offs. Decisions may take longer when we step back to question assumptions. Heightened concern can feel inefficient in moments of calm. Yet these costs pale against the benefits of early intervention. Discovery of small problems before they become significant helps avoid bigger issues and crises.

Organizations closing feedback loops within 48 hours see a 40% increase in near-miss reporting. Robust upward communication leads to a 30% reduction in incidents.

This discussion will be explored more fully in Chapter 9.

Technology and Human Judgment

Technology can amplify our vigilance but never replace it. Real-time fatigue monitors, dashboards, and automated trend detectors enhance our perception. Ultimately, though, human judgment is needed to assess the underlying assumptions of any alert. Cultivating persistent unease involves teaching groups to spot biases such as normalization of deviance or optimism bias, viewing each standard job as a chance to learn. After a close call—whether a child's scraped knee or a machine's unexpected vibration—we pause, map the contributing factors, implement improvements, and circle back to verify their effectiveness.

Fostering a Culture of Respect

Above all, chronic unease thrives in a culture of respect rather than fear. When leaders admit uncertainty, share mistakes, and encourage questions, they create psychological safety. Rituals such as morning huddles that begin with "What might we be missing today?" and monthly reflections that celebrate "red-flag" reports reinforce that unease is not paranoia but professional pride. In households and boardrooms alike, the same ethos applies caring enough to challenge complacency, vigilant enough to catch the weak signals, and humble enough to know we'll never see everything.

Daily integration of these practices at home and at work transforms chronic unease. It changes it from a passing worry into a cultural norm. It turns success into a prompt for scrutiny, calm into caution, and routine into a source of vital insight. Upcoming chapters detail real-world examples of how constant vigilance saves lives, from offshore platforms to ICUs. Complacency is dangerous; constant awareness is the best defense.

Chapter 8

Case Studies in Safety Leadership and Chronic Unease

❖

The actual power of concepts like safety leadership and chronic unease is revealed not in theory, but in practice. It is one thing to understand the principles—it is another to embed them into everyday operations, across shifts, teams, and disciplines.

This chapter presents a series of illustrative case studies, some of which are inspired by real-world events and organizations, and others partially fictionalized to underscore key themes. The intent is to explore how the principles of safety leadership and chronic unease manifest in high-risk environments— highlighting both success and failure—not to document or evaluate actual corporate conduct.

While some cases draw loosely on proper companies and events, details have been altered or fictionalized for illustrative purposes. Any resemblance to actual organizations, individuals, or occurrences is coincidental and intended solely to highlight critical learning points. These narratives illuminate how leadership, culture, and systems interact—and why every decision matters.

Case #1—DuPont's Strategic Transformation: Safety Leadership and the Discipline of Chronic Unease

DuPont's transformation from a compliance-focused organization to a benchmark in industrial safety leadership wasn't accidental. It stemmed from a deeply intentional cultural shift—one rooted in the understanding that safety isn't a static endpoint but a dynamic system of vigilance. The company's most revolutionary move was not merely treating safety as a moral or regulatory imperative but elevating it to a core strategic advantage—a driver of operational excellence, employee engagement, and corporate reputation.

At the heart of this transformation was the concept of chronic unease—a foundational mindset encouraging leaders and employees alike to challenge the assumption that "no news is good news." DuPont operationalized this unease as a strategic strength. Leaders were expected not just to monitor compliance metrics but to probe the spaces between them. Questions like "What might we be missing?" and "What assumptions could be wrong?" became routine. Curiosity became a corporate asset.

DuPont's success came from a deliberate restructuring of leadership accountability—not individual heroics. A Safety, Health, and Environment Committee, directly overseeing performance and cultural indicators, was established by the Board of Directors. This demonstrated top-level commitment to safety. The CEO reviewed all serious incidents and near misses monthly, establishing a "leadership safety rhythm" that cascaded throughout the organization.

Mid-level leadership underwent perhaps the most profound shift. Plant managers—traditionally evaluated on production and cost—had their compensation restructured, with 40% tied to safety culture indicators. Promotion decisions explicitly considered a leader's ability to foster chronic unease within their teams. An operations director explained their shift in focus: from promoting firefighters who reacted to problems, to elevating those who proactively prevented them. They described the latter as "almost paranoid about risks others couldn't yet see."

The leadership development pipeline was redesigned to identify and cultivate this mindset. High-potential leaders rotated through safety roles—not as a checkbox, but as a critical developmental experience. The message was clear: advancement required showed mastery of safety leadership principles.

Executives and plant leaders made floor walks a daily ritual— not as inspectors, but as engaged listeners. They asked questions, probed gently, and valued frontline feedback. A machine operator's gut feeling about a change in the hum of a pump wasn't dismissed—it was treated as a potential early warning. This approach fostered psychological safety. Employees felt trusted, not scrutinized.

To sustain chronic unease, leaders institutionalized a concept they called "cognitive dissonance by design"—a deliberate tension between comfort and vigilance. External safety experts were regularly invited to challenge assumptions. Safety reviews included skeptics and fresh eyes—those unconditioned to local norms—ensuring blind spots weren't overlooked.

Risk interpretation developed. Instead of relying solely on lagging indicators, DuPont prioritized weak signal detection. Slight process anomalies, uncharacteristic maintenance trends, and even minor housekeeping deviations were treated as early warnings of potential systemic failure. Chronic unease became a refusal to be soothed by green dashboards.

Perhaps most significantly, DuPont embedded this mindset into its governance architecture. Safety concerns bypassed hierarchy: operators were given direct access to senior leadership for urgent issues. Decision-making became precautionary by default: when in doubt, pause and investigate—don't proceed and hope.

The result? A culture where near-miss reporting soared—not because risk increased, but because trust did. Reporting was no longer seen as failure—it was foresight. Leaders rewarded transparency and humility. Admitting uncertainty became a sign of strength.

Importantly, this transformation extended beyond operations. DuPont infused chronic unease into engineering and innovation.

During project design, teams conducted "pre-mortems"—scenarios exploring how systems might fail before they were built. These weren't theoretical—they were grounded in operational reality and memory.

Over time, incidents declined, reliability improved, and retention increased. DuPont redefined safety leadership—not as a constraint, but as strategic capability. And chronic unease, far from being a liability, became one of its greatest assets.

Case #2—BP's Safety Reckoning: From Texas City to Macondo—The Fragile Arc of Cultural Transformation

The 2005 explosion at BP's Texas City refinery shattered more than just a furnace—it ruptured long-held assumptions about the depth to which safety must be embedded in a global enterprise. In its immediate aftermath, BP's leadership adopted the mantra "Listen, Learn, Lead," dispatching executives to the field for unscripted conversations with frontline workers. Investigators shifted focus from blame to root-cause analysis, and near-miss reports surged tenfold in pilot areas. For a moment, *chronic unease*—a disciplined discomfort that questions success rather than celebrates it—seemed to permeate the entire organization.

BP's initial response was marked by urgency and resolve. The CEO commissioned an independent review—the "Baker Panel"—with exceptional autonomy to examine not only technical failures but also systemic leadership shortcomings. This broke with precedent: previous inquiries seldom scrutinized executive decision-making.

The ensuing leadership cascade was broad and highly visible. The executive committee earmarked $1 billion for safety improvements—a symbolic figure underscoring the priority. Over 150 site visits followed in six months, not as audits, but as opportunities to listen.

At the governance level, the board restructured its committees, creating a Safety, Ethics, and Environmental Assurance Committee with access to operations data and the power to challenge investments on safety grounds. Compensation frameworks for the top 500 leaders were revised to include safety culture metrics, not just financial targets.

However, BP's matrixed structure revealed its fragile fault lines. On paper, safety teams in Houston and London reported to global functions regional operations managers in areas like the North Sea, Gulf of Mexico, and Alaska controlled budgets and schedules. When London's safety team recommended slowing maintenance to re-audit high-pressure vessels, the North Sea region quietly declined—citing tight quotas and the CEO's public pledge of "on-time delivery."

This gap—where formal authority clashed with operational reality—was a design flaw that undermined cultural reform.

Though well-meaning, the board's changes couldn't resolve the core tension between centralized safety expertise and decentralized operational control.

As one London-based director noted, "The safety team had good intentions, but our only lever was moral suasion. When the regional P&L owner says, 'We can't afford this delay,' talk of reform falls silent."

Beneath this power struggle, middle management emerged as a key fault line. While senior leaders voiced support for the new ethos, mid-level managers—often hired for cost discipline—viewed chronic unease as an obstacle. In Midland, Texas, one experienced manager admitted that near-miss data had become "just another metric to hit." Fearing scrutiny and budget cuts, he instructed staff to re-categorize hazards as general "maintenance backlog" issues, suppressing critical signals under corporate pressure.

The leadership development pipeline reinforced this contradiction. Despite new rhetoric, promotions continued to favor those who delivered on cost and production. An internal audit revealed that, of 87 management promotions in critical operational roles between 2006 and 2009, only three candidates had significant safety leadership experience. The message was unmistakable: safety might be mentioned, but financial delivery remained the true currency of advancement.

In the Gulf of Mexico, resistance surfaced among drilling engineers and site foremen. One junior engineer recalled logging a pressure bump in the riser during his shift handover. But when relayed to the drilling superintendent, the report was stripped of urgency. *"They simply omitted the qualifier 'urgent,'"* he said. *"By the time I followed up, operations had moved on—and my voice was drowned out by the sound of drills."*

This selective reporting took multiple forms:

- The "high-visibility exemption": Incidents were logged at marquee assets like Prudhoe Bay, while smaller fields quietly under-reported leaks.
- Truncated safety forums: Meetings became bullet-point briefings, steering clear of contentious issues.
- Metrics choreography: Regional directors manipulated dashboards to maintain "compliance" above audit thresholds.

When the Baker Panel released its findings, it described BP's culture as split in two: an ambitious, reform-driven group near headquarters and a pragmatic, "get-er-done" field contingent. The impact was uneven. Where leaders truly embodied *chronic unease*—spending time in the field, listening to concerns—near misses became catalysts for change. Elsewhere, the initiative faded into slogans, referenced in town halls but ignored in back-office decisions.

By April 2010, the Macondo well sat nearly two miles beneath the Gulf, surrounded by warning signs. Cement tests revealed unstable mixtures; negative pressure tests returned anomalies. A few rig workers raised concerns during a safety huddle, only to be told, "That's *a known quirk—move on.*" When a superintendent escalated the issue, his presentation was cut down, omitting critical data, as leadership rushed to approve a cost-saving plan.

The decision gate meeting, designed as a crucible for tough debate, lasted under 30 minutes. The regional VP, citing "project momentum" and bonus incentives, pushed for green lighting the operation. Two safety engineers objected in writing; their emails were ignored. One lead engineer kept asking, *"What are we missing?"*—only to hear, "Time *is money—we can't afford delays.*"

Macondo's failure wasn't merely technical—it was a breakdown of leadership and decision architecture. Safety voices were systematically marginalized. The structure prioritized schedules and cost over scrutiny and caution, reducing formal safety procedures to box-checking exercises.

Days later, the blowout and fire claimed eleven lives, unleashing the largest marine oil spill in U.S. history. Investigators found critical alarms were missed and documented anomalies were never acted upon.

The 2011 Chemical Safety Board report criticized BP for treating "safety as a program" instead of a mindset. Because cost-cutting became the priority, the very behaviors that had spurred reform after Texas City—field immersion, open dialogue, and vulnerability in decision rooms—disappeared. The report found no link between *chronic unease* and promotion criteria, compensation, or operations. Under pressure, the system reverted to expediency.

BP's second reckoning introduced sweeping reforms: independent oversight boards, a mandate for three-party risk reviews, and clear pay-performance ties for executives. Yet, the deeper lesson is this: incomplete transformation leads to relapse. A safety culture built on slogans cannot endure stress. Only persistent, systemic reinforcement—woven into governance, daily metrics, and decision-making—can sustain it.

For every leader, BP's journey carries a stark reminder: cultural change must be total, systemic, and unrelenting. It must outlive crises, resist budget cuts, and empower everyone—from rig hand to regional director—to question assumptions even in calm waters. Only then does *chronic unease* grown from a mantra into a way of life—a shield against complacency.

Case #3—Shell's North Sea Doctrine: Fusing Sensor and Soul in Safety Leadership

In the relentless theater of the North Sea—where machinery, weather, and time constantly collide—Shell's offshore crews aboard the Sea Guardian had long leaned on a fortress of automation. Sophisticated dashboards tracked every nuance of pressure, torque, and flow across the sub-sea architecture. In this domain, technical precision was the currency of safety. But on one storm-stirred morning, Shell's operational paradigm subtly but profoundly shifted—because of a single, almost casual human insight.

The system had done its job: it flagged a slight torque deviation in a sub-sea valve. Statistically insignificant, the alert was logged as a low priority. But just before sunrise, deckhand Lara McIntyre, sharp despite fatigue, radioed in a simple report: *"Valve felt stiffer than usual on manual override."* No alarms. Just a feeling.

That *feeling*—unmeasurable but unmistakable—triggered a cascade. Engineers, revisiting the flagged alert considering Lara's report, recognized the dissonance between what the system reported and what a human sensed. That tension became a signal of its own.

By midday, inspectors had pinpointed a corroded spindle, hidden by system redundancy but already compromising tactile performance. The readings weren't wrong—just incomplete. The failure lived in the blind spot between digits and instinct. By early afternoon, divers had replaced the part, turning what could have been a pressurized hydrocarbon release into routine maintenance.

Shell's leadership saw more than a lucky save—they saw a model. Safety wouldn't thrive against technology, but through its integration with human intuition. From this moment, Shell reframed its training doctrine, emphasizing that crews must not only read data but also share stories—valuing intuition even when it resists quantification.

This wasn't regression—it was evolution beyond digitization. Shell taught that data without narrative is a map without bearings. Lara's offhand comment—shaped by touch, memory, and experience—became a global case study. Shell's safety meetings developed into "story sessions," where crew members described what felt off: an odd vibration, a shifting pitch, a subtle resistance. These "soft signals" were cataloged alongside quantitative data—not as replacements, but as contextual amplifiers.

Out of this shift emerged a doctrine: Sensor and Soul—a leadership approach that embraced the limits of both machine and human and honored their union. Supervisors learned to pursue informal feedback, not dismiss it. Engineers were trained to ask: *"What feels different today?"* These weren't small talk—they were critical inputs.

Incident reviews were transformed, integrating narrative timelines of how events were perceived in real time by those on the ground. Shell embedded this ethos into its broader commitment to Chronic Unease: the belief that no signal, however subtle, should be ignored simply because it doesn't light up the screen.

Shell trained leaders to live in the productive tension between known and unknown, dashboards and gut, certainty and curiosity. This wasn't paranoia—it was vigilant humility.

The Sea Guardian incident ended not in failure, but in transformation. It reaffirmed that resilience lies not just in redundancy, but in a relationship—between data and dialogue, systems and senses, logic and lore. Shell's safety culture didn't grow by doubting technology—but by trusting the people who live alongside it.

Case #4 -Wood Group's Frontline Resolve: How One Pause Redefined Global Safety Leadership

In the mid-morning heat off Brazil's coast, where steel meets salt and the air smells faintly of aviation fuel, the helideck atop a Wood Group offshore platform hummed with focus. Crew members moved with practiced coordination, preparing for a routine medevac drill—rotor checks, manifest reviews, safety lines in place. It was a ballet in boiler suits.

At the edge of this rhythm stood José Silva, a roustabout just five years in, when he felt a pause—not in time, but in his gut. While prepping a load sling, he noticed a slight imbalance. The cargo's weight had shifted off-axis—only by a degree. In another moment, he might've dismissed it: wind, angle, chance. After all, drills were high stakes affairs and stopping them for a nuance could invite ridicule or rebuke.

But José had recently completed Stop Work Authority (SWA) training, not as a box-ticking formality, but as a cultural commandment. The core message: *"If you feel unsafe, not only may you stop work—you are expected to."* He remembered one line in particular: "Hesitation is insight. Speak it."

So he did.

He laid down his tools, calmly radioed the deck supervisor, and called for a pause. No drama. No panic. Just a signal of chronic unease—a quiet discomfort that might have been swallowed by routine. Supervisors responded swiftly. Upon inspection, they discovered a worn clevis pin, its metal beginning to shear under load. Not obvious. Not flagged. But left untouched, it might have failed mid-air, mid-lift, mid-life.

The near miss didn't escalate. Because José spoke.

His decision was quickly validated and celebrated. Word spread—not as a reprimand, but as a model of excellence. In the weeks that followed, his refined sling-inspection process was documented, reviewed, and implemented globally across Wood Group's offshore fleet.

At a town hall broadcast across continents, the Vice President said: "One degree of tilt, one voice of pause—that saved lives and millions in potential loss. That's safety leadership."

This wasn't just procedural change—it was a cultural pivot. Safety no longer belonged to management alone. It lived in every hand, every instinct. Empowerment moved from slogan to practice; Wood Group didn't just grant trust—it practiced it.

A new ethos of micro-courage emerged: the courage to raise concerns that seem too small to matter. Safety meetings began with frontline "sightings"—subtle anomalies turned teachable moments. Supervisors weren't just trained to respond, but to revere hesitation. *"What gave you pause?"* became a standard debrief question.

Most importantly, Chronic Unease matured into a leadership virtue. Crews were taught to maintain a respectful suspicion of the familiar. An offshore mantra emerged: "Nothing is too minor. Nothing is too early." This discipline—a fusion of humility, vigilance, and permission—turned every platform into a radar for the invisible.

Today, José Silva's story is part of every new hire's onboarding—not because it ended in heroism, but because it prevented it. His lesson: leadership isn't always in stripes or titles—it's in gloves, torque checks, and listening to instinct.

In a world where operational tempo often outpaces caution, Wood Group redefined the equation: one degree, one person, one decision—can bend the arc toward resilience.

Case #5 -Fukushima Daiichi's Defiant Hours: Improvisation, Unease, and the Leadership of Last Resort

At 3:36 p.m. on March 12, 2011, a thunderous roar shattered the sky above Fukushima Daiichi. Hydrogen, trapped by failed venting systems, ignited above Reactor 1—blasting away steel cladding and launching concrete shards skyward. The tsunami minutes earlier had already drowned the backup generators; control-room displays went dark; pumps meant to cool the reactor cores stood still. Decades of engineered safeguards had collapsed, and plant superintendent Masao Yoshida found himself in an uncharted sea of risk.

Yoshida's first move was radical pragmatism: he ordered fire trucks—designed for land fires—to pump raw seawater into the reactor vessels. Every engineer knew seawater spelled corrosion: valves would seize, pipes degrade, and decommissioning would become exponentially harder. But hesitation meant meltdown.

As one engineer later put it: *"We chose equipment sacrifice over human sacrifice."*

Next came the car-battery hack during the Chernobyl incident case. Teams scavenged ten 12-volt batteries from the parking lot, wiring them together to power emergency valves. The concept worked—until voltage surges charred valve motors, producing sparks in radiation zones. Operators, shielded and anxious, exchanged minutes of cooling for minutes of exposure.

Yet every act of heroism carried hidden costs. On March 13, an improvised pump line ruptured at a weak coupling. Seawater flooded a substation, tripping one of the last active power buses and disabling a secondary cooling loop. Four precious hours were lost to rewiring. One supervisor admitted: *"We were building our way out of collapse, but every fix could become a new failure."*

Flashlights taped to helmets pierced the darkness—but also cast harsh shadows. Several workers tripped over debris, sidelining them when the workforce was most vital.

Beyond the technical minefield was a deeper moral tension. Every workaround demanded operators take life-altering risks, often with uncertain outcomes. When a junior engineer questioned whether seawater might exacerbate hydrogen buildup, Yoshida hesitated. *"In those seconds,"* he later said, *"I felt the weight of every life downstream."*

Once the crisis stabilized, investigations hailed these improvised tactics as the thin line between meltdown and survival. But they also issued clear warnings: improvisation is no substitute for robust design. Crisis-driven hacks demand equally rigorous after-action reviews.

Today, Japan's nuclear sector has embedded the "Yoshida Scenarios" into core training. Drill scripts now simulate Level-Zero Loss events: no power, no instrumentation, cascading failures. These drills also include hack-failure simulations:

- A mock pump that bursts under pressure.
- A simulated arc forcing shutdown.
- An improvised valve fix that creates a new leak.

Crews learn not only how to invent solutions, but how to recognize when to abort them—before a fix becomes a fault.

Fukushima's lesson isn't blind praise for improvisation. It's a layered parable of tension between ingenuity and restraint:

1. Technical debt: Seawater saved the cores but crippled long-term systems.
2. Labour exposure: Improvised work raised radiation risks—some workers required long-term health care.
3. Organizational memory: Lacking proper documentation, many post-crisis innovations faded—until Yoshida Scenarios revived them in training.

True safety leadership, Fukushima shows, lives in adaptive rigor—a discipline that:

- Maps failure modes before deploying a hack.
- Weighs exposure versus time gained, with escalation protocols.
- Documents every step—successful or not—for future learning.

Above all, it embraces the humility to say: *"I may save lives today, but I might plant tomorrow's risk."* That is the crucible where chronic unease is truly forged.

In the end, Fukushima Daiichi did more than expose nuclear vulnerability—it illuminated the complex calculus of improvisation. It left behind not a rulebook, but a blueprint for balanced resilience—one that celebrates human ingenuity yet always remembers the cost it may carry.

Case #6 -Kashagan's Quiet Pivot: Unease, Engineering, and the Courage to Rebuild Before First Oil

In the windswept northern Caspian, where sea and sky blur into a single, icy horizon, the Kashagan project rose like a monument—an engineering marvel of ambition and scale. Artificial islands bore massive processing trains gleaming beneath the Caspian sun. This was one of the most complex offshore oil ventures ever attempted. And it nearly launched with a catastrophic design flaw.

With the project well advanced in engineering and construction, Aisha Karim, a junior process engineer, ran a routine dispersion model during a late QA review. One simulation stopped her cold: under rare but plausible wind conditions, a hydrogen sulfide (H_2S) release from one train could drift toward maintenance corridors on the adjacent train. The probability? Low. The consequence? Lethal.

Vent stacks were already being installed. Architectural plans were locked. Raising this now meant delaying a multi-billion-dollar operation. But Aisha couldn't ignore it. What she carried wasn't proof—it was chronic unease, born not from certainty, but from a refusal to trust silence over risk.

"Do you understand what you're asking?" The operations director's voice cut through the room like ice. "With so much progress. The board is committed. You want to revisit the layout based on a theoretical model?"

Under twenty senior executives' scrutiny, Aisha stood her ground. *"Yes, sir. That's exactly what I'm asking."*

Pushback followed—intense and personal:

- "The probability is negligible."
- "We've passed every regulation."
- "This will cost millions."

Even her division lead faltered. For several agonizing weeks, Aisha endured resistance, dismissals, and subtle isolation. *"You're burning your career,"* a colleague warned. Her data was questioned, dissected, and deemed overcautious.

At night, she imagined the alternative—staying silent. She pictured maintenance crews in those corridors. She saw faces. Families. Funerals.

At the final board meeting, H_2S risks earned one slide, marked *"mitigated by protocols."* When the chairman asked for closing comments, Aisha rose.

Her voice steady, she held up a document: "This is the emergency response plan for a Level 3 H_2S release. It routes evacuations directly through the zone with my model flags." Then she added, "Page two lists the names of twenty-seven workers assigned to those corridors."

Silence. Then the CEO spoke: "We don't gamble with lives. Not even at long odds."

In a rare decision, the consortium approved a last-stage redesign. The trains were relocated 150 meters apart. Vent stacks were re-engineered. The cost: more than \$100 million. The delay: significant. But for Aisha, the fallout was personal—ostracism, stalled career paths, performance reviews hinting at "poor team orientation."

Then, years later, during a standard turnaround, H_2S sensors in the new buffer zone flickered red—trace levels, but real. Wind matched Aisha's model. Sirens sounded. Twenty-two workers evacuated calmly via newly established routes. No one was harmed. But everyone remembered.

That evening, the operations director approached Aisha. No speeches. Just a hand on her shoulder. *"Twenty-seven people,"* he said. *"Twenty-seven families who'll never know how close it came."*

The Kashagan leadership's decision to listen—to act on unease, not just acknowledge it—became a landmark in safety culture. Aisha wasn't a senior executive. She wasn't a project lead. She was simply the right voice in the right room, with the courage to challenge momentum.

In an industry driven by scale, speed, and cost, Kashagan's pivot remains a rare moment of ethical engineering, where success was defined not by barrels or budgets, but by breaths still drawn by workers who never knew how close they came to not coming home.

Case #7 -The Crane Barge Near-Miss: One Voice, One Echo, One Saved Dock

The drydock was quiet that morning-quiet in the way only shipyards can be, filled with distant clangs and the echo of salt-laced wind brushing steel. Towering above it all stood the crane barge Resolute, a 3,000-ton colossus undergoing routine maintenance trials. Below, welders ticked at seams, inspectors reviewed checklists, and preparations hummed for a massive 2,500-ton module scheduled for lift within days.

But atop the barge, inside the operator's cab, Henrik Larsen prepared for a mid-capacity trial run with the focus of a man who had lifted not just metal, but entire lives with his decisions. With over thirty years of offshore lift experience, Henrik had learned the language of machines-the tremors, groans, and tones that most ears ignored. He was fluent in mechanical unease.

The test lift was uneventful. The load swayed gently in the breeze. Monitors read green across the board. But then, as the winch reeled, a faint chirp-a high-pitched metallic ping-cut through the usual drone. Just once. Then again. Not loud. Not obvious. But enough to snag Henrik's thoughts like a splinter.

To an untrained operator, it might have been brushed off as ambient noise: maybe a loose shackle, maybe a gust echoing off steel. But Henrik had learned to listen not just to the machine, but to the part of himself that didn't trust silence dressed as normalcy.

Henrik's hand hovered over the radio. Through the cab window, he could see the dock supervisor checking his watch, the client representative speaking animatedly into a phone, the construction manager reviewing the day's critical timeline. The module was scheduled for installation in just 48 hours-a narrow window aligned with weather predictions, tide patterns, and three support vessels from offshore. Delaying now would trigger a cascade of postponements, contract penalties, and costs running into the hundreds of thousands per hour.

Just then, his radio crackled. "Henrik, how's it looking up there? We need to complete three more test lifts before noon to stay on schedule."

He stared at the monitors. All green. All normal. Just that ping-that tiny, almost imperceptible ping. Maybe it was nothing. Probably it was nothing. In thirty years, how many false alarms had made him pause, only to find everything in order?

His thumb pressed the transmit button. "*I heard something.*"

Silence. Then: "*Can you be more specific?*"

"*A ping from the sheave assembly. Could be nothing.*"

The radio crackled again, this time with the voice of the client rep: "*Henrik, the installation vessel is costing us $340,000 a day. If you're confident the systems are nominal, we need to proceed.*"

Sweat beaded on his forehead despite the cool morning air. This was the moment-the moment where experience battled doubt, where chronic unease faced down operational pressure. He thought of all the times he'd been wrong before, all the delays he'd caused that revealed nothing. He thought of his reputation, his standing among the crew.

Then he thought of the module's weight-2,500 tons of steel that would hang from these very cables in two days' time. He thought of the sixteen men who would work directly beneath it, the additional thirty-seven in adjacent zones. Their faces flashed before him-many he knew by name, had shared meals within the mess, had swapped stories about children and grandchildren.

Henrik made his choice.

He cut power.

"*Full stop,*" he radioed, his voice firm. "*I'm calling for an immediate inspection of the sheave assembly. Something's not right.*"

The silence that followed was deafening.

"*Henrik,*" came the superintendent's voice, razor-edged, "*do you understand what you're doing here? This is a critical path item. We've got vessels on route, we've got weather closing in, we've got-*"

"*I understand,*" Henrik interrupted, something he rarely did. "*But I'm not moving this crane until the sheave assembly is inspected. Not one meter further.*"

The superintendent's voice rose. "*Based on what? A feeling? A hunch? Do you have any actual data suggesting a problem?*"

Henrik closed his eyes. "*No. Just thirty years of listening to machines tell me when they're about to fail. And this one is whispering.*"

What followed was the longest four hours of Henrik's career. The yard manager arrived, red-faced and demanding explanations. The client threatened to invoke penalty clauses. Fellow operators gave him sidelong glances-some sympathetic, others questioning his judgment.

"*You realize what you're doing to our schedule? To our reputation?*" the yard manager demanded during a tense meeting in the control room.

"*Yes,*" Henrik said simply. "*And I'll take full responsibility if I'm wrong.*"

Finally, reluctantly, the teardown was authorized. A team of engineers began dismantling the pulley sheave system-the core rigging element that had passed inspection only days earlier.

The lead engineer's voice broke through the crackling radio four hours later. "*Henrik? You need to get down here. Now.*"

When Henrik arrived at the inspection area, a crowd had already gathered. In the center, laid out on a tarp, was the partially disassembled sheave. The engineer handed him a flashlight and pointed to a nearly invisible hairline crack running along the interior bearing housing.

"*Subcranial fracture*," the engineer explained, voice hushed. "*Completely invisible to standard inspection. Under normal load, it held. But under the stress of a 2,500-ton module...*" He didn't finish the sentence. He didn't need to.

Computer modeling, conducted overnight, confirmed what everyone now understood with gut-wrenching clarity: under the planned lift conditions, the sheave would have catastrophically failed approximately 70 seconds into the main lift-precisely when the module would have been suspended directly over the crowded work zone.

"*How many?*" Henrik asked, his voice barely audible.

"*Simulations suggest complete structural failure*," the engineer replied. "*Given the positioning and personnel assignments scheduled for the lift...*" He swallowed hard. "*Minimum casualty estimate is forty-three workers. Maximum is sixty-eight.*"

The yard fell silent. Work halted. Men removed their hard hats. Some made calls to family members. Others simply stared at the fractured piece of metal that had nearly caused the largest industrial disaster in the yard's history.

The sheave was swapped out. The Resolute resumed trials four days later. And when the time finally came to lift the module-six days behind schedule but with a fully inspected and reinforced system-it was as if nothing had happened.

Because nothing had.

When word spread of how close they had come to catastrophe-and how it had been averted by a sound only Henrik had registered-the atmosphere in the yard changed. Men who had once scoffed at what they called Henrik's "excessive caution" sought his advice. Apprentices asked to shadow him during operations. The company instituted a formal review of its inspection protocols, identifying seven additional critical components requiring enhanced testing beyond current industry standards.

At a company-wide meeting two weeks later, the yard manager who had once berated Henrik stood before the assembled workers. His usual bluster was gone.

"I want to address the recent events surrounding the Resolute," he began. *"Some of you know we came... very close... to a significant incident."* His voice caught. He cleared his throat. *"I owe Henrik Larsen a personal apology. And I owe this yard something more important-a commitment."*

That day, the company formalized its "One Voice Authority" policy-a directive empowering any team member, from apprentice to senior operator, to halt operations if something felt off. It was a radical move in an industry long governed by hierarchy and momentum.

Six months later, a junior electrician used that policy to stop work on a different vessel when she noticed an unusual vibration in a primary generator. Inspection revealed critical insulation failure that could have resulted in an electrical fire in a confined space. When asked how she had known to report it, she said simply, "*I remembered Henrik's story. I remembered the echo in the steel.*"

The story is now used in operator schools, onboarding programs, and high-risk site briefings. Trainees are taught that machines speak-and that only those who listen past the volume hear what matters most.

Most importantly, they learn that volumes of regulations and mountains of procedures cannot replace the most valuable safety tool: a human being with the courage to trust their unease and the organizational support to act on it.

In an industry obsessed with metrics and milestones, the greatest success often lies in disasters that never happen in future headlines that never need to be written, in emergency sirens that never sound, in grief that never needs to be experienced.

The Resolute lifts on. Its legacy isn't just in the modules it moves, but in the unseen fracture it never lets fall-and in the lives that continued, unknowing but unbroken, because one man refused to ignore the echo in the steel.

Case #8 -The Offshore Separator Explosion: The Price of a Deferred Instinct

At twilight, the platform floated against the Gulf's darkening horizon—an industrial silhouette in fading light. As the day cooled, the night crew gathered around an aging, rust-marked gas-oil separator, long overdue for overhaul. The job was standard routine, but not without risk. The separator was connected to a sister platform kilometers away. Per work permits, the interconnecting pipeline was blind-flanged—isolated, inert, sterile.

On paper, everything was perfect.

But as the team prepared, Samira Patel, the lead technician, hesitated.

She'd done dozens of these jobs. She knew the signatures of gas—the hush of pressure bleeds, the feel of cold pipe skin under gloved fingers. And something here felt off. The line, supposedly dead, seemed to breathe.

She suggested direct verification of the blind flange—a two-hour trip, stakeholder reapproval, and logistical delays. Supervisors pushed back. *"The paperwork's in order."* *"You'll delay everything."* One even added, *"Don't make this harder than it needs to be."*

Samira relented—but uneasily. She ordered extra caution. And the night deepened.

Miles away, on the sister platform, operators faced a process upset. Needing to relieve pressure, they rerouted gas. Unknowingly, they sent it surging down the supposed deadline. The flange had failed—through error, miscommunication, or both.

There were no alarms. No sounds. Just gas—pressurized, invisible—moving toward the maintenance crew.

And then—a spark.

The explosion tore through the deck. The separator ruptured like a tin can. Fire engulfed the bay. Seven lives were lost. Dozens were injured. Scars, both physical and procedural, were left behind.

In the investigation, logs were analyzed, protocols dissected. But one phrase emerged—spoken by Samira Patel hours after the flames were extinguished:

"I knew we should've walked those flanges."

Those eight words became a refrain—more than regret: a revolution.

The incident sparked sweeping changes. Remote verifications were banned. Dual-site, physical verification of isolations became mandatory. New checklists now ask, *"Have you walked the line? Have you touched the flange?"* Training programs now teach that unease alone is sufficient to stop the job.

Leadership culture shifted. Supervisors now learn to recognize not only technical risks, but the value of hesitancy as expertise. Toolbox talks include a new final prompt: *"Does anything feel off?"*

Samira stayed in the industry. Her voice—once dismissed—is now central to high-stakes training. Her story is retold in every offshore orientation. Now a leading signal, her instinct has evolved from background noise.

The offshore separator explosion is a tragedy etched in pain, but its legacy is measured in lives saved by procedures born of unease. It reminds us that safety cannot live solely in documents—it must live in people, in pauses, in the courage to question what seems routine.

Across platforms and refineries, stories like Samira's have crystalized a single truth: Safety is not a destination—it is a dialogue. A tension. A system powered by trust in those who speak when something doesn't feel right.

Because sometimes, a whisper—if heard—can be louder than an alarm.

Case #9 — Piper Alpha (North Sea, July 6–7, 1988): Complacency Beneath the Flame

When Piper Alpha first began production in December 1976, it was designed as an oil-only platform—its high-pressure equipment tucked safely away from living quarters and control rooms. In 1980, however, a decision was made to convert Piper Alpha into a combined oil-and-gas production facility. This retrofit placed gas-compression modules and condensate-handling systems near personnel areas, fundamentally eroding the passive safety barriers that had once separated hydrocarbons from human life. By mid-1988, Piper Alpha was the busiest platform in the North Sea, processing over 300,000 barrels of oil per day and handling large volumes of high-pressure condensate.

On the evening of July 6, maintenance crews prepared to overhaul Condensate Pump A. To facilitate recertification, the pump's pressure safety valve (PSV 504) was removed and replaced with a blind flange—a temporary disk intended to isolate the line. Crucially, this flange was only hand-tightened, with no torque verification and no formal secondary inspection. The permit-to-work (PTW) form included a handwritten instruction: "Pump A must not be started under any circumstances." However, this warning was not effectively communicated to the incoming day shift. When the morning crew—unaware that PSV 504 had been removed—started Pump A, the hand-tightened flange failed under pressure. An estimated eighty kilograms of condensate gas erupted onto the deck and ignited almost instantly.

The resulting explosion ripped through Module C, obliterating both pump modules and rupturing adjacent gas and condensate pipelines. Flames rapidly spread to the main condensate riser, which in turn collapsed onto neighboring modules, feeding the fire for hours. Attempts to activate the emergency fire-water pumps were thwarted when control systems were disabled by the blast; manual activation also failed due to intense heat and structural damage. Meanwhile, the Offshore Installation Manager (OIM) delayed ordering a full evacuation, awaiting explicit onshore clearance rather than treating an uncontrolled hydrocarbon release as grounds for immediate abandonment. Dozens of personnel remained in the central accommodation block—exposed to smoke inhalation, inhalant toxins, and collapsing structures—resulting in 167 fatalities and scores of injuries.

In November 1990, Lord Cullen's Inquiry established that Piper Alpha's disaster was neither unforeseeable nor purely technical. Instead, it was the culmination of layered human and organizational failures:

- **Permit-to-Work Breakdown**: PTW procedures lacked a rigorous cross-check mechanism. The warning about Pump A's missing PSV was not effectively relayed, and no physical verification of the blind flange was ever performed. Without a second signature or confirmation of zero energy, the permit looked complete on paper but functioned as a lethal permission slip.

- **Eroded Inherent Safety**: Converting Piper Alpha to dual oil-and-gas operations placed gas-compression equipment beside control rooms and living quarters. High-pressure lines ran beneath personnel decks, transforming a design that once isolated hazards into one that allowed a single point of failure to cascade platform-wide.

- **Deficient Emergency Authority**: The OIM's authority to order an immediate evacuation was constrained by company culture and onshore-first protocols. Delays in evacuation decisions deprived many personnel of any chance to escape.

- **Weak Safety Culture**: Production targets and cost efficiencies frequently outweighed safety considerations. Near misses were seldom reported or examined, and frontline workers felt disempowered to halt operations even when they sensed something was amiss.

The Inquiry's 106 recommendations fundamentally reshaped offshore regulation in the United Kingdom. In 1992, the Offshore Installations (Safety Case) Regulations came into force, requiring every UK-licensed platform to maintain an up-to-date safety case demonstrating ongoing hazard identification, risk evaluation, and control measures anchored by a genuine culture of vigilance.

From a safety-leadership perspective, Piper Alpha highlights how complacency thrives when passive safeguards are allowed to age unchallenged and where leadership fails to reinforce the discipline of chronic unease. Had on-site leaders insisted on a secondary physical inspection of every isolation point, questioned the wisdom of clustering gas equipment next to living quarters, or granted the OIM the indisputable authority to evacuate without seeking remote approval, the disaster could have been averted. Instead, the platform's design alterations, coupled with a permit-to-work system that existed in name only, created a blind spot far too large to ignore.

Piper Alpha's legacy endures as a stark illustration that safety leadership must be more than a slogan: it must actively erode complacency at every level. A culture of chronic unease—where workers are encouraged to challenge apparent normalcy, where permits demand peer verification, and where evacuation authority is unquestioned—remains the only reliable safeguard against failures that begin as small oversights but end in unimaginable loss.

Closing Reflection: Story as Survival—And the Demands of Chronic Unease

While some cases in this chapter may echo familiar events or organizations, they should be understood as educational constructs—designed to highlight essential behaviors, decision dilemmas, and the transformative power of chronic unease. These are not accurate historical accounts, but they are narrative tools built from real lessons learned across many industries over time.

These stories are not just memories—they are survival tools. They provoke thought, deepen understanding, and inspire leaders at all levels to remain alert, humble, and courageous in the face of uncertainty.

Lessons Across Cases: What Safety Leadership and Chronic Unease Demand

Each narrative reveals timeless truths about leading safely when normalcy masks danger and certainty is a myth:

Visible Leadership Anchors Safety. The strongest safety cultures are built by leaders who show up—not just for inspections, but in silence, during shifts, in the field. Leadership isn't position—it's presence.

Chronic Unease Is a Leadership Discipline. The most impactful leaders don't wait for incidents. They invite discomfort during calm, asking *"What are we missing?"* not out of fear, but from strategic humility.

Culture Overrides Checklists. Procedures matter. But without a culture that welcomes dissent, questions, and hesitation, procedures are hollow. Safety thrives where every voice matters.

Emotions Are Signals, Not Distractions. Instinct, doubt, and unease are not noise—they're data. Much life-saving actions began with a feeling, not a reading. Leadership must make room for intuition beside instrumentation.

Empowered Voices Prevent Silence-Driven Failures. In every averted crisis, someone spoke—and someone in power listened. Empowerment isn't symbolic. It's operationally designed to let even a whisper halt momentum.

Learning Must Be Vigilant, Not Passive. Resilient organizations don't wait for disasters to learn. They investigate success as rigorously as failure and treat every task as a live test of their systems.

The takeaway is simple yet urgent: Safety isn't a state—it's a behavior. And chronic unease, practiced as a leadership discipline, becomes the quiet force that protects people, exposes blind spots, and keeps organizations truly alive.

Chapter 9

Embedding Safety Leadership at All Levels

❈

Embedding safety leadership across all levels of an organization demands more than policies and programs—it requires a living, relentless commitment that permeates routines, relationships, and decisions. True safety leadership ignites when executives, supervisors, frontline teams, and contractors alike feel not only empowered but obligated to speak up, collaborate, and innovate in pursuit of zero harm.

This chapter explores how to make that vision a reality—drawing on research, real-world successes, and practical strategies to speed up progress.

When upward communication channels are strong, workers speak frankly about hazards—before they become incidents.

> Research shows that organizations with such communication channels experience roughly 30% fewer safety events.

Leaders can increase this effect by engaging directly with operations. Methods include safety walks, listening tours, or an open-door policy, all signaling that leadership cares and that employee input matters.

But raising concerns is only half the equation. Closing feedback loops swiftly—ideally within 48 hours—boosts near-miss reporting by nearly 40% (National Safety Council). When employees see their input led to tangible change—a revised procedure, added guardrail, or upgraded gear—they gain trust in the system and engage more fully.

Supervisors are the linchpin. Their daily visibility turns policy into practice. Whether pausing work to spotlight a hazard, thanking someone for adjusting a task, or high five a safe lift, small actions make safety real. These micro-recognitions reinforce that safety is not a layer—it's core to every task.

Frontline workers uphold safety not just by compliance, but through active participation. Scenario-based drills and immersive simulations sharpen hazard recognition. Peer accountability builds courage—when one person speaks up, they grant others permission to do the same. Involving teams in PPE selection—trialing gloves or helmets, for example—can raise compliance from under 70% to over 90%, because the solution becomes theirs.

Contractors and temporary workers often operate at the cultural margins, yet account for up to 40% of high-severity incidents. To close that gap:

- Start with joint inductions, led by both client and contractor safety leads.
- Pair contractors with permanent-staff mentors.
- Include them in reporting, recognition, and learning forums to build shared ownership from day one.

Across every group, several universal practices reinforce a cohesive safety culture:

- Empower "safety ambassadors" at every level—trained in coaching and facilitation—to cascade best practices.
- Transform walkarounds into conversations: Start with *"What's working well? What's your biggest concern?"*
- Host storytelling sessions—moments when vigilance made the difference, or when a minor oversight taught a major lesson. These humanize safety and remind us why protocols exist.

Use visual tools—dashboards, boards, digital displays—to highlight trends, near misses, and shout-outs. Embed daily huddles, weekly "learning lunches," and quarterly "learning festivals" for shared reflection and recognition.

Finally, measure what matters. Go beyond lagging indicators and focus on leading signals.

- Hazard observations
- Safety participation rates
- Corrective-action closure times

- Psychological safety (via anonymous surveys)

Use this data not to punish—but to improve, sharing trends transparently, celebrating progress, and collaborating on dips.

Cultural change is a long game—three to five years, on average—and demands consistency. Leaders must resist the temptation to declare victory too soon. Instead, they recommit through setbacks, adapt with challenges, and stay present through every shift.

When safety becomes woven into daily conversation, recognition, storytelling, and data, organizations develop—from having a safety program to having safety as part of their identity.

And when everyone—from the CEO to the newest hire—sees care and vigilance as part of their role, safety leadership doesn't need enforcing. It lives and breathes on its own.

To embed chronic unease across an organization, several practices have proven especially effective:

- **Leader-led walkarounds:** Leaders engage with frontline staff not just to inspect, but to inquire. They ask, *"What concerns you?"* and *"What's changed recently?"*—surfacing weak signals before they harden into threats.

- **Scenario planning:** Teams regularly explore unlikely but high-consequence events. Structured *"What if?"*

exercises stretch assumptions, sharpen imagination, and build operational resilience.

- **Near-miss storytelling:** Rather than filing reports and moving on, teams revisit near-misses through structured storytelling. These narratives convey context, emotion, and decision-making under pressure—making the lessons memorable and actionable.

- **Open forums and listening sessions:** Employees are encouraged to speak openly about concerns, confusion, and unease. Leaders respond not with judgment, but with gratitude and action, reinforcing a culture where hesitation signals wisdom, not weakness.

- **Cognitive training and bias interruption:** Organizations invest in critical thinking workshops that address heuristic traps, challenge overconfidence, and promote reflective judgment. Teams learn to pause, question, and detect the creeping onset of complacency.

- **Peer activation and social permission:** Peer-to-peer accountability amplifies vigilance. When one person speaks up, it normalizes the behavior and grants others permission to do the same, creating a self-sustaining safety net.

- **Respond promptly and let people know what's happening:** When employees see their concerns lead to visible change—within 48 hours where possible—reporting rates rise, and trust in the process deepens.

Metrics matter, too. Mature organizations don't just track outcomes—they monitor leading indicators of vigilance:

- Near-miss reporting rates
- Volume and quality of safety suggestions
- Frequency of "what if" drills and scenario testing
- Participation in safety dialogues
- Psychological safety scores from anonymous feedback

Together, these practices don't just sustain awareness—they cultivate a mindset of active vigilance. When chronic unease is embraced as a leadership value rather than a sign of instability, organizations shift from reacting to expecting. Safety, then, becomes not a goal to check off, but a continuous, lived commitment—one that sharpens attention, deepens trust, and ultimately, saves lives.

In the next chapter, we shift from organizational systems to you—the individual leader—and how to carry this mindset forward in every decision you make.

Chapter 10

Sustaining the Momentum — Making Safety Leadership Enduring

⚜

Creating and sustaining a culture of safety leadership takes more than a campaign or a surge of enthusiasm. It requires a way of being—one where vigilance and care are embedded in every task, conversation, and decision. Too often, safety initiatives launch with energy, only to fade when new priorities emerge or supports move on.

To endure, safety must be woven so deeply into daily life that it thrives even when no one is watching. That means turning every success, near miss, and lesson learned into fuel for the next improvement.

Imagine ending each week not with relief that nothing went wrong, but with curiosity:

- What did we learn?
- What caught us off guard?
- Where did our good intentions nearly fall short?

When teams ask these questions regularly—in informal huddles, three-question check-ins, or conversations over coffee—they transform routine into reflection. Over time, this habit of

141

learning becomes the organization's heartbeat—steady, reliable, and strong.

The vision that guides us must not become a plaque on the wall. It must be renewed, revisited, and reimagined to reflect emerging risks, developing challenges, and the people bringing it to life. When executives, supervisors, and frontline workers gather to honor progress, confront new questions, and recommit, the energy becomes shared—and sustained.

Yet energy alone isn't enough. Recognition is the spark that keeps vigilance alive.

- A leader pausing mid-shift to thank a technician who spotted a hidden hazard.
- A team celebrating the near miss that could have become a tragedy.
- A peer-nominated award for someone whose quiet diligence saved a colleague.

These moments of acknowledgment reinforce that safety isn't a checklist—it's a lived value.

Cultures built on a few passionate supports are fragile. To last, leadership must be passed on—intentionally. When high-potential employees shadowy senior leaders serve on safety committees, or lead key initiatives, they form an unbroken chain of stewardship. When transitions happen, successors don't scramble—they're ready.

Safety must also infuse the core systems of the business:

- In capital project planning, risk is weighed alongside return.
- In onboarding, cultural immersion matters as much as compliance.
- In performance reviews, safe behaviors are celebrated like results.

When safety is embedded in how the business defines success, it's no longer extra—it's essential.

Metrics guide the journey. Beyond past incidents, leading indicators shine a light forward:

- Near-miss reporting volume
- Frequency of safety conversations
- Corrective-action closure rates
- Psychological safety scores

These aren't used for blame—they're beacons for focus. When displayed openly in meeting rooms and dashboards, they become a shared language of improvement.

As organizations strengthen, so must our methods. From VR walkthroughs and gamified hazard hunts to peer-led Safety Labs (†), innovation keeps learning alive. When people see their ideas tested and scaled, they take ownership of the safety challenge.

In the end, what makes safety endure is not compliance—it's identity. We become the people who care—not because rules demand it, but because that's who we are.

When leaders share why safety matters to them—protecting family, honoring a mentor, keeping a promise—they invite others to make it personal. One company asks every new hire to write a letter to their future self—a personal safety pledge. A year later, they read it aloud. The commitment deepens.

Rituals anchor the culture: daily briefings, monthly recognitions, annual reflections. Symbols—like posters, dashboards, and awards—remind us of shared values. But none of this thrives without vulnerability. When leaders admit uncertainty, share their missteps, and ask for input, they open space for trust.

That's when safety transforms—from rules and checklists into a web of relationships: between teams, across functions, and between leaders and those they serve.

Bringing It Home: Personal Actions to Sustain Safety Leadership

To make your safety leadership enduring—not just organizational but personal—consider taking one or more of these concrete steps:

1. **Write Your Own Safety Pledge.** Set aside a moment—today or this week—to draft a brief letter to your future self. Describe the safety behaviors you'll model, the

conversations you'll spark, and the values you won't compromise. Save it in an email draft or seal it in an envelope. Set a calendar reminder to reopen it in six months.

2. **Build a Weekly Reflection Habit.** Block 15 minutes at the end of each week to journal on three questions:

   - What went well?
   - What surprised me?
   - Where did I almost miss something?

   Use these insights to shape the week ahead. Share one reflection with your team or a colleague. Small reflections create lasting awareness.

3. **Lead with Vulnerability in Your Next Meeting.** Open your next team meeting, huddle, or 1-on-1 by sharing when you missed a hazard—or made a mistake—and what you learned. Then invite others to share. Modeling candor unlocks trust.

4. **Champion a Safety Conversation Buddy System.** Pair up with a colleague and check in monthly. Ask about hazards, near-misses, or improvement ideas. Rotate buddies each quarter. It's a simple structure that keeps vigilance fresh and distributed.

5. **Integrate Safety into Your Personal Goals.** Add one safety-focused aim to your personal development plan. It could be:

- An advanced safety course was finished
- Mentoring a junior colleague in hazard recognition
- Testing a new engagement activity. When safety lives in your goals, it stays on your radar—not the margins.

By choosing one—or several—of these actions, you bring this chapter's ideas into motion. You move from theory to practice, and you carry the momentum forward—not just as a leader of others, but as someone who models what it means to care.

As this chapter closes, remember: sustaining momentum is not about one more campaign—it's about keeping the conversation alive.

It's choosing:

- Curiosity over complacency
- Trust over fear
- Renewal over resignation

Because safety leadership is not a task to complete—it's a commitment to live.

And at its heart, safety is personal. It endures when we choose to care.

(†) *VR walkthroughs* use Virtual Reality to simulate real-world hazards, allowing workers to practice identifying risks in a safe, interactive environment. *Gamified hazard hunts* are game-based challenges that encourage teams to spot and report potential dangers competitively. *Peer-led Safety Labs* are informal, employee-run forums where teams share safety innovations, lessons learned and lead collaborative problem-solving.

Supplemental Chapter

Resilience and Accountability in Safety Leadership

Co-written by Taehee Kim and Nelson Oliveros

❖

The Dual Challenges of Safety Leadership

Safety leadership in hazardous industries is a demanding role, requiring leaders to balance the critical responsibilities of protecting workers and ensuring compliance within complex systems. These leaders often experience immense stress due to high-stakes decision-making, constant vigilance, and the pressures of blame culture.

This chapter explores two essential dimensions of effective safety leadership: cultivating personal resilience and fostering organizational accountability. Together, these approaches empower leaders to navigate their roles with clarity and emotional stability. Dr. Taehee Kim, a specialist in mindfulness-based leadership development, offers insights from neuroscience and contemplative practices to demonstrate how mindfulness can enhance performance, emotional regulation, and ethical responsibility under chronic pressure.

Understanding the Pressure

Leaders in high-risk environments must make rapid, high-stakes decisions under intense pressure. Neuroscientific research shows that acute stress activates the amygdala—responsible for fear and emotional response—which, in turn, suppresses the Pre-Frontal Cortex (PFC), the region responsible for rational thinking and executive control (Arnsten, 2009). This neurological shift, often referred to as "amygdala hijack," impairs a leader's ability to process information calmly and effectively.

Mindfulness meditation, particularly Focused Attention Meditation (FAM), has been shown to counteract these effects. Tang et al. (2007) demonstrated that just five days of mindfulness training enhanced connectivity between the Anterior Cingulate Cortex (ACC) and the Dorsolateral PFC (dlPFC), improving emotional regulation and attention control. In a broader review, Tang, Hölzel, and Posner (2015) found that mindfulness reduces amygdala reactivity and strengthens regulatory networks, thereby supporting resilience.

Physiological evidence further supports these findings. Farb et al. (2015) reported that mindfulness practice enhances interoceptive awareness through increased activation of the insular cortex. This, in turn, improves emotional regulation and supports autonomic recovery after stress exposure, as reflected in improved Heart Rate Variability (HRV).

Key Insight: Brief, consistent meditation—such as 10 minutes of breath-focused practice daily—can help safety leaders maintain executive function, regulate emotional responses, and foster cognitive clarity in challenging environments.

The Role of Accountability in Shaping Culture

In many organizations, unclear accountability frameworks contribute to the development of blame cultures—environments in which individuals are held personally responsible for systemic failures. This culture undermines psychological safety and stifles innovation, open communication, and collective learning.

Establishing robust accountability systems is essential. Frameworks such as ISO 45003:2021 provide structured approaches for identifying and mitigating psychosocial risks in the workplace. These include guidance on leadership responsibility, role clarity, and organizational transparency—all of which influence how responsibility is perceived and shared.

Mindfulness can support cultural transformation by enhancing self-awareness and reducing defensive behaviors. Neuroscientific research shows that mindfulness activates the brain's default mode network (DMN), which is associated with introspection and metacognition (Brewer et al., 2011). This network allows individuals to observe their thoughts without immediate judgment—an essential skill for navigating accountability conversations.

Additionally, functional imaging studies have shown that Loving-Kindness Meditation (LKM) increases activation in the insular cortex, a region linked to empathy and perspective-taking. Klimecki et al. (2014) found that individuals who practiced LKM exhibited enhanced prosocial responses and improved emotion regulation—both critical for constructive, team-based accountability.

Practical Applications:

- Incorporating 2-minute mindfulness check-ins before team meetings can create space for reflection and reduce reactivity.
- Encouraging leaders to keep reflective journals fosters metacognitive awareness and supports the development of non-defensive responsibility.
- Promoting regular dialogues focused on system-based inquiry (e.g., "What conditions led to this?" rather than "Who is at fault?") helps shift the organizational mindset from blame to shared responsibility.

Building Resilience Through Mindfulness

Resilience in safety leadership goes beyond mere endurance; it refers to the capacity to recover swiftly and respond adaptively to high-pressure situations. Neuroscience provides growing evidence that mindfulness practices enhance this capacity by modulating both physiological and cognitive stress responses.

One well-studied technique is body scan meditation, which enhances interoceptive awareness—the ability to perceive internal bodily states—by increasing activity in the insular cortex. Farb et al. (2015) found that this practice improves emotional regulation by enabling individuals to detect and interpret subtle stress signals earlier, leading to more effective self-regulation.

Cognitive flexibility is another cornerstone of resilience. Open Monitoring Meditation (OMM), which encourages non-reactive awareness of changing experiences, has been linked to enhanced theta wave activity in the frontal lobe. This activity supports attentional switching and real-time evaluation. Slagter et al. (2007) reported that individuals trained in OMM demonstrated more efficient allocation of limited attentional resources, enhancing performance under pressure.

Although individual responses vary, research consistently shows that mindfulness reduces autonomic arousal and supports recovery. Benefits include improved sleep, reduced baseline anxiety, and increased Heart Rate Variability (HRV)—a biomarker of nervous system adaptability.

Practical Applications:

- Safety leaders may benefit from regular body scan or open monitoring practices to improve baseline emotional resilience.
- A post-incident mindfulness protocol (e.g., 5 minutes of quiet reflection or breath awareness) can help recalibrate stress responses and reduce the risk of long-term exhaustion or trauma.
- Organizational support for mindfulness education contributes to a culture where recovery and reflection are institutionalized, not merely encouraged.

Effectively integrating mindfulness into leadership development requires alignment across behaviors, systems, and organizational culture. While mindfulness is often viewed as a personal wellness tool, research increasingly supports its value in enhancing professional performance and team dynamics—especially in high-stress environments.

Micro-practices, such as short breathing pauses during shift transitions, offer low-barrier entry points. These brief interventions support attention regulation and stress reset without demanding significant time. Cognitive science shows that intentional breaks can enhance memory consolidation and reduce attentional fatigue (Baumeister & Tierney, 2011).

Digital tools, including apps like Headspace for Work or Calm Business, provide structured, scalable mindfulness content. These platforms use evidence-based design and behavioral reinforcement to sustain engagement—especially when supported by leadership endorsement.

Equally important is leadership modeling. When executives and managers openly practice or discuss mindfulness, they establish social norms that encourage participation. Neuroscientific research on mirror neurons suggests such modeling fosters prosocial imitation and emotional alignment within teams.

To address skepticism, organizations can present neurobiological evidence. For example, long-term meditators exhibit increased gamma wave activity, a pattern linked to heightened awareness and integration (Lutz et al., 2004). When paired with performance metrics—such as reductions in errors, absenteeism, or burnout—these findings help reposition mindfulness as a strategic advantage rather than a soft skill.

Practical Applications:

- Introduce 3-minute breathing pauses at the beginning or end of team briefings.
- Use app-based mindfulness programs during onboarding or leadership development.
- Encourage leaders to share personal experiences with mindfulness in psychologically safe settings.

- Present neuroscience-informed rationales to gain buy-in from analytical or results-oriented teams.

A Vision for the Future

As safety leadership continues to evolve, mindfulness is increasingly positioned as a core competency rather than a supplementary skill. The convergence of neuroscience, occupational psychology, and leadership science suggests a future where inner stability is as essential as technical expertise.

Emerging technologies, such as neurofeedback-enhanced meditation, offer promising new directions. By using Electroencephalogram (EEG) based tools to monitor brainwave patterns in real time, leaders may soon tailor mindfulness training to their individual cognitive and emotional profiles— maximizing the effectiveness and impact of resilience development.

Organizational standards are also adapting. ISO 45003:2021, the first global standard focused on psychosocial risk, urges employers to treat emotional well-being as a key component of workplace safety. When integrated with mindfulness initiatives, such frameworks can help reduce systemic stressors and foster a culture rooted in accountability and care.

Afterwords

At a personal and basic level, whenever I visit the yard or site, I draw on a chronic-unease mindset—opening each safety intervention with my proven five-question framework:

1. What are you doing?
2. What hazards are present?
3. What controls do you have in place?
4. How would an accident affect you personally?
5. How would it affect your family?

Repeatedly, this simple approach transforms routine checks into deeply meaningful conversations: workers feel that leaders genuinely care about them, and they leave each interaction with renewed conviction that they—and their families—deserve to return home safely at the end of every shift.

While this book closes here, the journey of refining your mindset continues. Think of these pages as the first step—one that invites you to return, explore new case studies, and deepen your practice in future volumes. The conversation on resilience, accountability, and the power of disciplined curiosity is just beginning.

Nelson Oliveros

References

Chapter 1

1. Conklin, T. (2012). *Pre-Accident Investigations: An Introduction to Organizational Safety*. Ashgate Publishing.

2. UK Health and Safety Executive (HSE). (2021). *Developing and Maintaining Safety Culture*.

3. Dekker, S. (2014). *The Field Guide to Understanding 'Human Error'*. CRC Press.

4. Edmondson, A. (2019). *The Fearless Organization: Creating Psychological Safety in the Workplace*. Wiley.

5. Hopkins, A. (2009). *Failure to Learn: The BP Texas City Refinery Disaster*. CCH Australia.

6. National Safety Council. (2022). *Workplace Injury Statistics*.

7. Weick, K. & Sutcliffe, K. (2015). *Managing the Unexpected: Sustained Performance in a Complex World*. Wiley.

8. Interviews with petrochemical safety leaders (2018–2023)

Chapter 2

9.   Baker Panel Report. (2007). *The report of the BP U.S. Refineries Independent Safety Review Panel.*

10.   Dekker, S. (2016). *Just culture: Restoring trust and accountability in your organization.* CRC Press.

11.   Edmondson, A. (2018). *The fearless organization: Creating psychological safety in the workplace for learning, innovation, and growth.* Wiley.

12.   Fernández-Muñiz, B., et al. (2019). "Safety culture elements and relationships: A meta-analysis." *Safety Science, 118,* 221-232.

13.   Hopkins, A. (2005). *Safety, culture and risk: The organizational causes of disasters.* CCH Australia.

14.   O'Neill, P., & Schultz, W. (2013). *The leadership journey at Alcoa.* Harvard Business Review Press.

15.   Reason, J. (1997). *Managing the risks of organizational accidents.* Ashgate.

    Fruhen, L., Flin, R., & McLeod, R. (2013). Chronic unease for safety in managers: a conceptualization. Safety Science, 57, 92-98.

16.   Flin, R. (2021). Safety Leadership: Chronic unease: A state of mind to manage safety risks. Safety+Health Magazine.

17. Dekra. (n.d.). What is Chronic Unease? - A State of Mind to Manage Safety Risks. University of Western Australia research summary.

18. NHS England. (2022). Safety culture: learning from best practice.

19. Flin, R., & Fruhen, L. (2015). Managing Safety: Ambiguous Information and Chronic Unease. Safety Science.

20. Risktec. (2023). Chronic unease – the hidden ingredient in successful safety leadership?

21. Long, I. (2018). My Top 20 Safety, Leadership, and Coaching Books. LinkedIn Article.

22. Reason, J. (1997). Managing the risks of organisational accidents. Ashgate Publishing.

23. Weick, K. E., & Sutcliffe, K. M. (2001). Managing the Unexpected: Assuring High Performance in an Age of Complexity. Jossey-Bass.

24. Hackitt, J. (2013). Process safety, focusing on what really matters – leadership. UK Government Review.

Chapter 3

25. International Association of Oil & Gas Producers. (2022). *Transparency in Safety Reporting.*

26. National Safety Council. (2021). *The Impact of Safety Vision on Employee Engagement.*

27. Health and Safety Executive. (2021). *Underreporting in Pathological Safety Cultures.*

28. Journal of Safety Research. (2020). *The Sustainability of Reactive Safety Measures.*

29. Deloitte. (2023). *Safety Culture and Bureaucracy Survey.*

30. American Society of Safety Professionals. (2022). *Proactive Safety Metrics.*

31. Massachusetts Institute of Technology. (2022). *Generative Cultures and Organizational Performance.*

32. Institution of Occupational Safety and Health. (2023). *Comparative Analysis of Safety Maturity Models.*

33. Gallup. (2021). *Communication Channels and Safety Reporting.*

34. Harvard Business Review. (2023). *Reflective Practices in Safety Management.*

Chapter 4

35. Peterson, J. B. (2018). *12 Rules for Life: An Antidote to Chaos*. Random House Canada.

36. *Cited for leadership philosophy and the importance of integrity.*

37. DuPont. (2008). *The Bradley Curve: A Model for Cultural Evolution*. DuPont Sustainable Solutions.

38. *Referenced for the Bradley Curve framework in tracking safety culture progression.*

39. BP. (2010). *Post-Texas City: BP's Global Leadership Program on Risk Literacy and Emotional Intelligence.* BP Safety & Operational Risk Reports.

40. *Cited for BP's post-incident cultural reforms.*

41. Shell. (2015). *Real-Time Safety Dashboards: Integrating Data for Proactive Decision-Making.* Shell Global Safety Publications.

42. *Referenced for Shell's use of real-time safety analytics.*

43. Wood Group. (2017). *Decentralizing Safety Ownership: The Role of Safety Champions in Project Teams.* Wood Group White Paper.

44. *Cited for embedding safety champions in operations.*

45. NASA. (2003). *Columbia Accident Investigation Board (CAIB) Report.* U.S. Government Printing Office.

46. *Referenced for NASA's cultural shift post-Columbia disaster.*

47. ISO. (2018). *ISO 45001: Occupational Health and Safety Management Systems—Requirements with Guidance for Use.* International Organization for Standardization.

48. *Cited for the framework aligning safety culture with measurable outcomes (mentioned in the transition to the next chapter).*

49. Hopkins, A. (2009). *Failure to Learn: The BP Texas City Refinery Disaster.* CCH Australia.

50.   *Relevant for case studies on safety culture failures and reforms.*

51.   Reason,   J. (1997). *Managing   the   Risks   of Organizational Accidents.* Ashgate.

52.   *Cited   for   concepts   like   "chronic   unease"   and organizational resilience.*

53.   Geller, E. S. (2001). *The Psychology of Safety Handbook.* CRC Press.

54.   *Referenced for behavioral safety, feedback mechanisms, and positive reinforcement.*

55.   Hale, A., & Borys, D. (2013). *Working   to   Rule   or Working Safely? Part 1: The Management of Safety Rules and Procedures.* Safety Science, 55, 207-221.

56.   *Relevant for discussions on procedural compliance vs. cultural engagement.*

57.   Kahneman, D. (2011). *Thinking, Fast and Slow.* Farrar, Straus and Giroux.

58.   *Cited for cognitive biases affecting risk perception and decision-making in safety cultures*

Chapter 5

59.   National   Safety   Council   (NSC).   (2022). *Integrating Safety Metrics into Business Performance.*

60.   Occupational Safety and Health Administration (OSHA). (2021). *The Impact of Worker Involvement in Safety Planning.*

61. International Association of Oil & Gas Producers (IOGP). (2020). *Transparent Evaluation Processes in SMS*.

62. McKinsey & Company. (2023). *Predictive Analytics in Safety Management*.

63. Harvard Business Review. (2022). *Leadership Engagement in Safety Initiatives*.

64. Chemical Safety Board (CSB). (2021). *Chronic Unease and Process Safety Performance*.

65. Alcoa. (2019). *ISO 45001 Implementation Case Study*.

66. BP. (2020). *Interactive Training and Human Error Reduction*.

Chapter 6

67. U.S. Chemical Safety Board. (2014). Investigation Report: Macondo Well Deepwater Horizon Blowout.

68. Reason, J. (1997). Managing the Risks of Organizational Accidents. Ashgate.

69. Weick, K. E., & Sutcliffe, K. M. (2001). Managing the Unexpected: Resilient Performance in an Age of Uncertainty. Jossey-Bass.

70. Hopkins, A. (2012). Disastrous Decisions: The Human and Organisational Causes of the Gulf of Mexico Blowout. CCH Australia.

71. Rodríguez, J. A. (2018). Process Safety Leadership: Lessons from High-Reliability Organizations. Energy Press.

Chapter 7

72. International Civil Aviation Organization (ICAO). (2024). Annual Safety Report.
73. Reason, J. (1997). Managing the Risks of Organizational Accidents. Ashgate.
74. Weick, K. E., & Sutcliffe, K. M. (2007). Managing the Unexpected: Resilient Performance in an Age of Uncertainty. Jossey-Bass.
75. Dekker, S. (2011). Drift into Failure: From Hunting Broken Components to Understanding Complex Systems. CRC Press.
76. Fruhen, P., Flin, R., & McLeod, K. (2014). Psychological Traits Underpinning Chronic Unease in Safety-critical Environments.

Chapter 8

77. Reason, J. (1997). Managing the Risks of Organizational Accidents. Ashgate.
78. Dekker, S. (2014). The Field Guide to Understanding 'Human Error'. Ashgate.

79. Weick, K. E., & Sutcliffe, K. M. (2007). Managing the Unexpected: Resilient Performance in an Age of Uncertainty (2nd ed.). Wiley.

80. Turner, B. A. (1978). Man-Made Disasters. Wykeham Publications.

81. Hopkins, A. (2009). Failure to Learn: The BP Texas City Refinery Disaster. CCH Australia.

82. National Aeronautics and Space Administration (NASA) (1986). Report of the Presidential Commission on the Space Shuttle Challenger Accident.

83. International Atomic Energy Agency (IAEA) (2015). The Fukushima Daiichi Accident: Report by the Director General.

84. DuPont (2003). DuPont Safety Philosophy: Core Principles and Practices. Internal publication.

85. Pidgeon, N., & O'Leary, M. (2000). Man-Made Disasters: Why Technology and Organizations (Sometimes) Fail. Safety Science, 34 (1-3), 15–30.

86. Snook, S. A. (2000). Friendly Fire: The Accidental Shootdown of U.S. Black Hawks over Northern Iraq. Princeton University Press.

87. Health and Safety Executive (UK) (HSE). (2013). Human Factors in Health and Safety.

88. High Reliability Organization Council (HRO Council). (2018). Principles of High Reliability: A Toolkit for Safety Leaders.

89. BP (2007). The Texas City Refinery Explosion: Report by the BP US Refineries Independent Safety Review Panel (Baker Panel Report).

Chapter 9

90. Hofmann, D. A., Burke, M. J., & Zohar, D. (2017). 100 years of occupational safety research: From basic protections and work analysis to a multilevel view of workplace safety and risk. *Journal of Applied Psychology*, 102(3), 375–388.

91. National Safety Council. (2020). *Closing the Loop: Enhancing Safety Through Feedback.*

92. Occupational Safety and Health Administration (OSHA). (2021). *Improving Safety Culture Through Supervisor Engagement.*

93. Safety Science. (2022). *The Impact of Structured Safety Dialogues on Incident Rates. Safety Science Journal*, 135, 105–112.

94. National Institute for Occupational Safety and Health (NIOSH). (2021). *Advancements in Scenario-Based Training for Hazard Recognition.* Retrieved from NIOSH website.

95. Geller, E. S. (2019). *The Psychology of Safety Handbook.* CRC Press.

96. Journal of Occupational Safety. (2020). *Worker Involvement in PPE Selection Increases Compliance. Journal of Occupational Safety*, 45(2), 89–95.

97. Safety & Health Practitioner. (2021). *Joint Safety Inductions Reduce Contractor Incidents.*

98. Process Safety Progress. (2023). *Leadership Walkarounds: From Inspection to Engagement. Process Safety Progress*, 42(1), 23–30.

99. Kotter, J. P. (2012). *Leading Change.* Harvard Business Review Press.

100. Cullen, W. D. (Lord Cullen). (1990). *The Public Inquiry into the Piper Alpha Disaster: Report of the Court of Inquiry* (Cm 1310). London: HMSO.

101. Heath, B. (2008). *Piper Alpha: The True Story of the World's Worst Offshore Disaster.* Barnsley, UK: Pen & Sword Maritime.

102. Health and Safety Executive (HSE). (1992). *Offshore Installations (Safety Case) Regulations 1992.* London: HSE Publications.

103. Department of Energy (U.K.). (1991). *Piper Alpha: Official Photographs and Diagrams.* London: HMSO.

104. Vinnem, J. E., & Utne, I. B. (2007). "Risk Analysis in the Offshore Oil and Gas Industry," in **DiNenno, P. J. (Ed.), *Encyclopedia of Fire Protection.* New York: John Wiley & Sons.

105. Kletz, T., & Amyotte, P. (2018). *Process Plants: A Handbook for Inherently Safer Design* (3rd ed.). Boca Raton, FL: CRC Press.

106. Hall, J., Robinson, A., & Wood, D. (1992). "Organizational Failures in Offshore Safety: Lessons from Piper Alpha," *Journal of Loss Prevention in the Process Industries,* 5(1), 1–12.

107. National Institute of Standards and Technology (NIST). (1992). *Engineering Failure Analysis: Piper Alpha Disaster*. Gaithersburg, MD: NIST Technical Report.

108. Jones, O., & van der Walt, J. (1995). "Learning from Disasters: Offshore Drilling Case Studies," in Paté-Cornell, M. E., & Fischhoff, B. (Eds.), *Assessment of Technological Risks and Uncertainties* (pp. 189–216). Dordrecht, The Netherlands: Kluwer Academic.

Chapter 10

109. Hofmann, D. A., Burke, M. J., & Zohar, D. (2017). 100 years of occupational safety research: From basic protections and work analysis to a multilevel view of workplace safety and risk. *Journal of Applied Psychology*, 102(3), 375–388.

110. National Safety Council. (2020). *Closing the Loop: Enhancing Safety Through Feedback*.

111. Occupational Safety and Health Administration (OSHA). (2021). *Improving Safety Culture Through Supervisor Engagement.*

112. Safety Science. (2022). The Impact of Structured Safety Dialogues on Incident Rates. Safety Science Journal, 135, 105–112.

113. National Institute for Occupational Safety and Health (NIOSH). (2021). *Advancements in Scenario-Based Training for Hazard Recognition.*

114. Geller, E. S. (2019). *The Psychology of Safety Handbook.* CRC Press.

115. Journal of Occupational Safety. (2020). Worker Involvement in PPE Selection Increases Compliance. Journal of Occupational Safety, 45(2), 89–95.

116. Safety & Health Practitioner. (2021). *Joint Safety Inductions Reduce Contractor Incidents.*

117. Process Safety Progress. (2023). Leadership Walkarounds: From Inspection to Engagement. Process Safety Progress, 42(1), 23–30.

118. Kotter, J. P. (2012). *Leading Change.* Harvard Business Review Press.

Supplemental Chapter

119. Arnsten, A. F. T. (2009). Stress signaling pathways that impair prefrontal cortex structure and function. *Nature Reviews Neuroscience*, 10(6), 410–422.

120. Baumeister, R. F., & Tierney, J. (2011). *Willpower: Rediscovering the Greatest Human Strength*. Penguin Press.

121. Brewer, J. A., Worhunsky, P. D., Gray, J. R., Tang, Y. Y., Weber, J., & Kober, H. (2011). Meditation experience is associated with differences in default mode network activity and connectivity. *Proceedings of the National Academy of Sciences*, 108(50), 20254–20259.

122. Farb, N. A. S., Segal, Z. V., & Anderson, A. K. (2015). Mindfulness meditation training alters cortical representations of interoceptive attention. *Social Cognitive and Affective Neuroscience*, 8(1), 15–26.

123. Klimecki, O. M., Leiberg, S., Ricard, M., & Singer, T. (2014). Differential pattern of functional brain plasticity after compassion and empathy training. *Social Cognitive and Affective Neuroscience*, 9(6), 873–879.

124. Lutz, A., Greischar, L. L., Rawlings, N. B., Ricard, M., & Davidson, R. J. (2004). Long-term meditators self-induce high-amplitude gamma synchrony during mental practice. *Proceedings of the National Academy of Sciences*, 101(46), 16369–16373.

125. Slagter, H. A., Lutz, A., Greischar, L. L., Francis, A. D., Nieuwenhuis, S., Davis, J. M., & Davidson, R. J. (2007). Mental training affects distribution of limited brain resources. *PLoS Biology*, 5(6), e138.

126. Tang, Y. Y., Hölzel, B. K., & Posner, M. I. (2015). The neuroscience of mindfulness meditation. *Nature Reviews Neuroscience*, 16(4), 213–225.

127. Tang, Y. Y., Ma, Y., Wang, J., Fan, Y., Feng, S., Lu, Q., ... & Posner, M. I. (2007). Short-term meditation training improves attention and self-regulation. *Proceedings of the National Academy of Sciences*, 104(43), 17152–17156.

About the Authors

Nelson Oliveros

Nelson Oliveros is a dynamic professional with a diverse background in engineering, project management, and leadership. With over three decades of experience, he has cultivated expertise in the fields of safety engineering and construction management, working on large-scale projects across various industries. His career has been defined by a commitment to innovation, problem-solving, and delivering results in complex environments.

Nelson holds two Master of Science degrees in Environmental and Process Safety Engineering from the University of Southern Illinois and the University of Sheffield, respectively, as well as several leadership certificates from the London School, showcasing his dedication to continuous improvement and operational excellence.

Throughout his career, Nelson has held key positions in prominent organizations, including leadership roles, and his work has spanned infrastructure development, energy systems, and sustainable solutions, reflecting his passion for contributing to transformative projects that impact the industry positively.

As an author, Nelson brings his wealth of knowledge and experience to the written word, offering readers unique insights into the intersection of technical expertise and human ingenuity. His writing is informed by real-world challenges and triumphs, providing valuable perspectives on leadership, innovation, and resilience.

In addition to his professional pursuits, Nelson is deeply committed to mentoring young professionals and fostering growth within his industry. He believes in the power of knowledge-sharing and collaboration to drive progress and create meaningful change.

Nelson currently resides in Houston with frequent work assignments in South Korea, where he continues to pursue his passions in leadership and construction while writing and inspiring others through his work.

Taehee Kim, Ph.D.

Dr. Taehee Kim received her Ph.D. in Philosophy from the Department of Buddhist Studies at Wonkwang University. Her doctoral research analyzed the yogic practices and metaphysical insights presented in the *Gorakṣavacanasaṃgraha*, a seminal text attributed to Gorakṣa widely regarded as the practical reformer of Haṭha Yoga. Through this analysis, she systematically organized the foundational doctrines of the Gorakṣa tradition within an academic framework.

She currently teaches "The Theory and Practice of Meditation" at the Department of Yoga Studies, Graduate School of East Asian Studies, Wonkwang University, and serves as a senior researcher at the Yoga Studies Institute of Wonkwang University. She also holds academic leadership positions as Chair of the Academic Committee of the Korean Yoga Society and Chair of the Academic and Publishing Committee at the Academy of Korean Thought and Culture.

Dr. Kim facilitates mindfulness-based meditation programs at institutions such as the Samsung Human Resources Development Center, supporting a wide range of participants including corporate professionals, adolescents, and children not only in cultivating emotional healing and psychological resilience, but also in strengthening mindfulness-based leadership grounded in neuroscience and psychology.

She works at the intersection of intellect and lived experience, sharing meditation not merely as a technique but as a living philosophy an approach that harmonizes theoretical depth with practical relevance and continues to guide her educational practice.